Courtesy of the author

About the Editor

JONAH GOLDBERG was the founding editor and is currently editor at large of *National Review Online*. He is a Pulitzer-nominated columnist for the *Los Angeles Times* and is a visiting fellow at the American Enterprise Institute. His column is carried by the *Chicago Tribune*, *New York Post*, *Dallas Morning News*, and scores of other papers. His first book, *Liberal Fascism*, was a number one *New York Times* and Amazon bestseller and was selected as the number one history book by Amazon readers. He is a member of *USA Today*'s board of contributors and previously served as a columnist for *The Times* of London, *Brill's Content*, and the *American Enterprise*. His writings have appeared in the *Washington Post*, *Wall Street Journal*, *Christian Science Monitor*, *Commentary*, and *The New Yorker*, among numerous other publications. He is a Fox News contributor. He lives in Washington, D.C., with his wife, Jessica Gavora, and their daughter.

PROUD

★ TO BE ★

RIGHT

ALSO BY JONAH GOLDBERG

Liberal Fascism: The Secret History of the American Left, from Mussolini to the Politics of Meaning

HARPER

NEW YORK • LONDON • TORONTO • SYDNEY

PROUD

★ TO BE ★

RIGHT

VOICES OF THE NEXT CONSERVATIVE GENERATION

Edited and with an Introduction by

JONAH GOLDBERG

HARPER

HarperCollins books may be purchased for educational, business, or sales promotional use. For information, please write: Special Markets Department, HarperCollins Publishers, 10 East 53rd Street, New York, NY 10022.

FIRST EDITION

Designed by Justin Dodd

Library of Congress Cataloging-in-Publication Data
Proud to be right : voices of the next conservative generation / edited and with an introduction by Jonah Goldberg. —1st Harper paperback.
p. cm.
ISBN 978-0-06-196573-9
1. Conservatism—United States. 2. Youth—Political activity—United States.
I. Goldberg, Jonah.
JC573.2.U6P77 2010
320.520973—dc22 2010011494

---

10 11 12 13 14 OV/RRD 10 9 8 7 6 5 4 3 2 1

CONTENTS

INTRODUCTION

Jonah Goldberg

Did you ever wonder why the best comedians are blacks, Canadians, and Jews?

The reason certainly can't be gleaned from the usual prisms of race, class, or the other familiar, politically correct standards used to identify the Coalition of the Oppressed. Jews are pretty wealthy (they live like Episcopalians but vote like Puerto Ricans, goes the famous line), blacks on average are not. Blacks are lagging in educational achievement while Jews are ahead of the curve. Jews and blacks may have a significant history of oppression and discrimination but the most you can say about the Canadians on this score is that they merely think they do.

And that fact might point to the answer. Blacks, Canadians, and Jews are, each in their own way, insider-outsiders. They share both a fascination with and alienation from mainstream American culture.

Comedians from these groups tend to have mastered their own subculture as well as the majority culture (if you like, you can throw gays into this mix as well). One doesn't need to study the profiles of Chris Rock, Michael Meyers, or Jon Stewart to understand that these folks absorbed popular culture from just outside the fishbowl. It's a visitor-from-Mars thing. Most jokes are funny when they illuminate unnoticed links, connections, meanings from common experiences ("Didja ever notice . . . ?", "It's funny because it's true!"). This critical distance need not be ironic, cynical, or fodder for mockery. Indeed, it is more often a source of love and a yearning to belong.

Now, you might be wondering what any of this has to do with conservatism. And my answer would be: a lot. I've visited scores of college campuses over the years and one of the things that you notice is that the best conservatives are, on average, simply sharper than the best liberals. Obviously, there are any number of exceptions to this. There are plenty of mule-headed Right-wingers and any number of insightful and interesting young liberals. But at the far-right tail of the bell curve, the conservative kids are just a bit, well, *better*—better at explaining and articulating their ideas, better at weighing their feelings against the facts, better at sticking to their principles despite pressure from both their peers and their professors.

I think the reason for this is that, like blacks, Jews, and Canadians, young conservatives—at least on college campuses—must master their own culture and learn to live in the majority culture. And, unlike blacks or gays (leave Canadians and Jews out of it), they cannot rely on condescending professors to cut them some slack. Few professors want to get crosswise with the cult of victimology. And that's what would happen if a professor violated the sumptuary laws of political correctness that manifest themselves as identity politics.

But conservative kids are fair game. Indeed, wrenching the conservatism out of students has been one of the top priorities for many professors for more than a generation now. Even before the New Left (now quite old, truth be told) launched its march through the institutions in the 1960s, progressive professors believed it was their mission to remold the young. Woodrow Wilson, as president of Princeton, insisted that the first duty of the educator was to make children as unlike their parents as possible.

And so, today conservative college students routinely find themselves in the crosshairs of the professors as well as their peers. This is often unfair, but there's also a Darwinian benefit. The best learning is Socratic. It comes from having your core views questioned and challenged. Even the sharpest liberal students get much of their college and high school education *passively*—because they already agree with what the professor has to say. Their prejudices are confirmed, not challenged. Not so with conservative students. They are reminded every day that they are slightly out of tune with the majority. They see things with their head cocked slightly to the side.

The same trend applies in nearly all intellectual vocations. In higher education, the media, government, and that vast but ill-defined vocation sometimes called the "helping professions," conservatives have to swim upstream. This makes things harder for them, but it also builds muscle.

I do not say this in order to curry sympathy. Too many conservatives are seduced by the narrative of victimization. While conservative complaints are often right on the merits—we are called racists, bigots, fools, fascists, etc. every day by those who control the commanding heights of the culture—whining about it too much is counterproductive. For starters, it concedes the authority of the liberal establishment to make such claims. Moreover, it encourages conservatives to internalize two unhealthy responses. The first is the burning desire to offend liberals just for kicks. There's nothing wrong with such playfulness when it has a point or in moderation, but too often it comes across as obnoxiousness for its own sake. The second response is the near opposite: what might be called a self-hating conservatism, where conservatives feel the need to apologize for being "old-fashioned" or are too eager to prove they "care" too. It is this instinct that gave birth to the abomination that was George W. Bush's "compassionate conservatism."

Which brings us to the point of this book. There is little that unites the entries in this collection beyond the obvious: this is a book of essays by young conservatives. Some are secular, many are religious. Some take great pride in being Republicans; for others, party affiliation is meaningless or an afterthought. Within the broad confines of the conservative label, the essays display a wide ideological and cultural diversity. But there is one more commonality to this collection: self-confidence.

By this I do not mean the cockiness of youth—though there is plenty of that, too—but the confidence that comes with fundamental acceptance. This is conservatism without apologies. Many of the contributors seem alienated from the Bush years and the Republican Party; a few, like James Poulos, seem equally repulsed by what he deems to be the corruption of the professional conservative movement (or perhaps that should be the professionalization of the corrupt conservative movement). But nearly all come to their conservatism for reasons that defy easy or familiar caricature.

In his essay, Poulos remarks that someone will one day write (but hopefully not publish) a book called "*Conservatives Are People Too.*" It's funny, because I once made a similar point. Almost exactly fourteen years ago from the moment I write these words (when I was the age of the contributors to this book), I reviewed for the *Wall Street Journal* an anthology of conservative writers edited by David Brooks, called *Backward and Upward: The New Conservative Writing*. In my review, I observed that "The real difficulty for conservatives today isn't persuading the American people that their solutions are worth trying. The tough slogging lies in persuading the American people that conservatives are, well, people." Brooks's book, I proclaimed, "is a rousing demonstration that many conservatives—contrary to the elite media's depiction of them—actually have a sense of humor, an optimistic spirit, and a grasp of the vast realm of human experience that lies outside the Beltway and its policy concerns."

If anything, the contributors to *Proud to Be Right* demonstrate this very point more than the contributors to *Upward and Backward* did. For starters, the essayists in *Proud to Be Right* are younger and far less well-established than were the bullpen of contributors to *Upward and Backward* (which was crammed with such ringers as Andrew Ferguson, John Podhoretz, David Frum, and Fred Barnes—already big names back then). Moreover, all of the essays in this book are original. They were solicited to offer a showcase for writers who do not yet have a megaphone, but might deserve one. That is why Ross Douthat, Ramesh Ponnuru, Matthew Continetti, Yuval Levin, Reihan Salam, Nicholas Schulz, Mary Katharine Hamm, and various other prominent young or younger conservative writers were not invited to contribute. For the record, the formula for determining whether someone counts as "young" is simple: Are they younger than me? (Again, for the record, I am forty years old as of this writing, though I don't look a day over fifty-two). Still, my editor Adam Bellow and I leaned heavily in favor of selecting contributors at the dawn of their careers. Most important, this volume was intended to show—rather than tell—that, in fact, conservatives *are* people, too.

In a sense, this volume demonstrates both the folly and wisdom of Albert Jay Nock. For those who don't know, Nock was something like John the Baptist to William F. Buckley's Jesus (admittedly, there are just too many problems with this analogy to enumerate here, but you get the point). Nock is considered a prophet by both the libertarian and the conservative branches of the American Right. The author of *Our Enemy the State*, Nock was the patron saint of the conservative insider-outsider. He was a complete misfit for his times, literally and figuratively. He wore a cape, lived a mysterious life, considered Belgium every bit as good a country to live in as the United States, and believed passionately that there was really no point in trying to change the world for the better.

Nock would have no use for today's tea parties or talk-radio Jeremiahs of the Right, but he would also scoff at Paul Krugman and roll his eyes at Barack Obama's talk of hope and change, for he denied that the state was the proper object of hope or a worthwhile agent of change. Moreover, he had contempt for the vast bulk of humanity, the "Neolithic mass" and those who spoke to them. In the dark, or at least darkening, age in which he believed himself to live (Nock died two weeks after Hiroshima), he cared only for "the Remnant"—a tiny slice of humanity he could describe but not locate. The best way to grasp this idea is to read his 1936 *Atlantic* essay "Isaiah's Job" (Google it the first chance you get). It is one of the oddest and most powerful essays in the history of conservatism. At the end of King Uzziah's reign in 740 B.C., the prophet Isaiah was tasked with warning the Jews of God's wrath. But, in Nock's rephrasing of the Biblical text, God included this disclaimer: "I suppose perhaps I ought to tell you that it won't do any good. The official class and their intelligentsia will turn up their noses at you and the masses will not even listen. They will all keep on in their own ways until they carry everything down to destruction, and you will probably be lucky if you get out with your life."

Isaiah asked why he should even bother, then. "Ah," the Lord said, "you do not get the point. There is a Remnant there that you know nothing about. They are obscure, unorganized, inarticulate, each one rubbing along as best he can. They need to be encouraged and braced up because when everything has gone completely to the dogs, they are the ones who will come back and build up a new society; and meanwhile, your preaching will reassure them and keep them hanging on. Your job is to take care of the Remnant, so be off now and set about it." For Nock, the Remnant was his audience. At times, the idea of the Remnant is unapologetically elitist, but in a thoroughly Jeffersonian way. The Remnant were not necessarily the "best and brightest," the most successful, the richest. Rather, they were those occupying the "substratum of right thinking and well doing" (in Matthew Arnold's words). "Two things you do know, and no more: First, that they exist; second, that they will find you. Except for these two certainties, working for the Remnant means working in impenetrable darkness."

It's no wonder that Nock is deeply admired by many leading liberals today (both the *New Republic*'s Frank Foer and the *New York Times*' Sam Tanenhaus revere him as perhaps the ideal conservative). Nock openly embraced the idea that he couldn't change anything. History was driven by forces too large to be affected by politics or punditry. Any revolution would result only in a new crop of exploiters and scoundrels eager to pick up where the deposed ones left off. So, Nock figured, why bother with politics? What more could today's liberals ask for from a conservative pundit? He had it all: wit, urbanity, eccentricity, combined with absolutely zero interest in getting in the way of liberal schemes.

William F. Buckley was hugely influenced by Nock, but nonetheless rejected this core message of Nockianism. He famously believed that it is sometimes necessary to stand athwart history, yelling *Stop!* And Buckley was right, not just on the need to get in the way of the Hegelian God-State, like a Tiananmen Square protestor in front of a column of tanks, but on the necessity of building on the Remnant, expanding it, cultivating it, turning it into a *movement*.

The contributors to this book represent both sides of this argument. Some seem to be perfectly happy as denizens of the Remnant doing good and thinking right, and leaving it at that. These Young Nockians are conservative because that is what one is by default when one does good and thinks right. But others are Young Buckleyites, fighting the good fight on the fight's own terms. Helen Rittelmeyer offers perhaps my favorite essay in this book, in no small part because the line between Nockianism and Buckleyism runs straight through her heart. She's a feisty scrapper who loves a good argument but rejects the argument that one should make good arguments. That's just great stuff. And after you read her essay, nominally about the aesthetics of smoking at Yale, you'll be able to see what I mean about how campus conservatives tend to be just a little bit better than their opponents.

There's something I should say, since my name is on this book: I am a great fan of young people getting involved in politics, but I am a sworn enemy of "youth politics." By that, I mean I loathe the cheap identity politics that says your ideas and arguments count more—or less—simply because of your demographic cohort. In particular, I consider the whole Rock-the-Vote shtick to be something of a Baby Boomer cargo cult whereby young and generally addle-pated losers dance and shout the way the aging hippies expect them to. At least Civil War reenactors make no claim on contemporary political or cultural controversies, whereas sixties reenactors consistently think they are making a serious contribution rather than repeating history as farce.

When I came to Washington as a young conservative working at the American Enterprise Institute (I'm back there now as a grown-up, by the way), "Generation X" was all the rage. Twentysomethings of my generation were the first to attempt to pry the Baby Boomers' mood-ring-wrapped fingers from the cultural steering wheel. The funny part was that the crowd of Baby Boomers parted like courtiers when the dauphin enters the room.

"Youth! Glorious Youth! Let us bask in the glow of thy idealism!" liberal editors and politicians seemed to say. The catch was that these midlife-crisis liberals expected "the Youth" to play their role, behave the way young people are *supposed* to behave: i.e., like passionate liberals. And guess what? A lot of young, ambitious people opted to play their assigned role. An even more ambitious cabal of twentysomethings gamed the system by exploiting Baby Boomer insecurities and their gauzy memories of not trusting anyone over thirty. These twentysomethings insisted that the liberal establishment couldn't possibly understand young people. So the oldsters needed translators, demographic Indian scouts who could decipher the lingo and guide them through the alien territories of contemporary youth.

It was a brilliant tactic; sixties nostalgia became an informal affirmative action program. The youth cult played perfectly into the assumptions and logic of identity politics: blacks, women, gays, the disabled, and—now—the "young" all deserve to be "heard," regardless of the merits of what they have to say. The problem—or one of many problems—I have with all this is that "the youth" are not members in the Coalition of the Oppressed. Indeed, "youth rights" do not exist, because "special rights" of any kind are a ruse created by the Progressives for their own purposes. "Youth rights" is a concept best thought of as a sponge for the lugubrious rage of a handful of precocious teens and twentysomethings who cannot find a more coherent vessel for their agenda.

More to the point, youth politics as defined in the mainstream media and on college campuses is largely a training exercise for why kids should, must, need to be liberal. The claim is that young people are supposed to be passionate activists and agitators, but activism and agitation are defined in purely Left-wing terms. This is why Left-wing campus groups can get away with "bullying," as Ben Shapiro calls it. Destroying property, shouting down speakers, and harassing fellow students without serious sanction is par for the course for Left-wing students. But when conservative students step even remotely out of line, it is a clear sign that they are nascent fascists in need of reeducation.

This state of affairs owes itself to the fact that the Left still controls the commanding heights of the culture and has written the story of the last fifty years. But it's worth at least acknowledging how much of that story is so much myth-making. For instance, young conservatives in the 1960s were arguably just as energetic as, if not more than, their ideological opponents. Young Americans for Freedom had roughly as many members as Students for a Democratic Society. YAF organized earlier, and perhaps better, than SDS. It was in 1960 that YAF convened in Sharon, Connecticut, to decide on its principles; SDS did not hold its famous conclave in Port Huron, Michigan, until two years later.

The differences between YAF and SDS are instructive. YAF was considerably more blue-collar than SDS. The SDS-ers were spoiled; indeed they admitted as much. And it was the YAF, not the SDS, who were more strident, more apocalyptic, at least at first. The opening line of the Sharon Statement—the YAF charter—reads: "In this time of moral and political crisis, it is the responsibility of the youth of America to affirm certain eternal truths." The Port Huron Statement, meanwhile, begins with a certain lazy honesty about its self-indulgence: "We are people of this generation, bred in at least modest comfort, housed now in universities, looking uncomfortably to the world we inherit."

Moreover, the YAF-ers were unapologetic and unashamed to take direction from their elders (it was written at and issued from William F. Buckley's home in Sharon, Connecticut, and the lead author was a twenty-six-year-old M. Stanton Evans). Because conservatives understand that they are standing on the shoulders of giants and inheritors of a tradition that transcends themselves, the YAF-ers didn't need to make up a lot of soul-searching twaddle. The full Sharon Statement runs a mere 370 words, barely two pages of double-spaced type. Meanwhile, the logorrheic SDS-ers rambled on for more than 50 pages (the current edition of *The Port Huron Statement* runs some 160 pages, according to Amazon).

Hopefully, the only logorrhea you encounter in this collection is the stuff you just had to wade through by me. All I ask of the reader is to avoid looking for some easy theme to slap on this book. Adam and I did not solicit essays to fulfill our preconceived expectations; we did not ask our writers to play a role. We merely expected them to illuminate the experiences and attitudes of the next generation of conservatives. The results sometimes surprised us. I don't agree with every perspective in this book, and I know that not every contributor agrees with me on every issue. Indeed, the strength of conservatism for the last three-quarters of a century has been its disagreements, not its agreements. Conservative dogma remains as unsettled today as it was a generation ago. The question of where to draw the line between freedom and order, liberty and justice, the individual and the community, continues to fuel intense disputes. There really is no party line anymore.

Conservatism is too large for that sort of thing now; it is a culture unto itself, with all of the disagreements that define robust and healthy cultures. In a sense, that is the only thing to take away from this collection—for conservatives are people, too.

PROUD
★ TO BE ★
RIGHT

1

THE POLITICS OF AUTHENTICITY

Matthew Lee Anderson

Before there was Sarah Palin, there was Mike Huckabee.

Because the folksy governor of Arkansas has been eclipsed by the equally folksy governor of Alaska, it is easy to forget that Mike Huckabee was once the most electrifying and energizing candidate in a crowded field of Republican presidential hopefuls. Huckabee, who now has his own TV show on the Fox News channel, came from nowhere to make the primary a three-way race between himself, Mitt Romney, and John McCain.

The story of that rise really begins at a single event, the Values Voter Summit, which was hosted in October 2007 by the socially conservative Family Research Council. It is clear to me as someone who switched from interested observer to ardent Huckabee supporter after that event that the 2007 Values Voter Summit encapsulated many of the virtues and vices of the social conservative movement, and the interesting relationship social conservatives have with the rest of the Republican Party.

Like many social conservatives, I entered the presidential primary season of 2007 uncertain whom to pull the lever for. Social conservatives were simultaneously terrified by the prospect—which seems laughable now—of another Clinton presidency, and infuriated by the Republican establishment's decision to appoint Rudy Giuliani the presumptive front-runner. With a number of Supreme Court justices potentially retiring during the next term, and with the wave of backlash building against President Bush, social conservatives were anxious that the gains they had made (and they had made some) during the Bush years would be rolled back. We were looking for a leader, and one hadn't yet emerged.

Sam Brownback was supposed to be our shining light, but he ran an uninspiring race and was gone before the serious campaigning began. John McCain was . . . John McCain, and he clearly wasn't going to win an election. As much as my friends all liked Fred Thompson's snarky YouTube video calling out liberal filmmaker Michael Moore, he had no apparent interest in actually being president.

Our best chance was, therefore, Mitt Romney, who seemed to have the complete package: he had the money, the looks, and the rhetoric, and had demonstrated that he could win elections. He had won the governorship in Massachusetts and had taken the Ames Straw Poll—which takes social conservatives' temperature—in the summer of 2007 by a landslide.

It was in this context that I made my way to the Family Research Council's Values Voter Summit.

In any other year, the summit would have been largely irrelevant. But with all of the Republican candidates scheduled to attend, and a straw poll at the end of the weekend, it had been hyped as a sort of derby for the social conservative vote. Which is precisely what it turned out to be.

The Values Voter Summit is, admittedly, an odd affair. There is a blatant mixing of patriotic sentiment and religious fervor. Yet as disconcerting as this might be to some, most attendants are reasonable, honest, and, frankly, not very scary people who care more about cultural values than they do about Christianizing the government per se—as muckraking reporter Max Blumenthal found out when he attempted to "expose" the seedy underbelly of the event, only to produce a video with mostly benign and inoffensive interviews. The event was indeed permeated by a conscious anxiety about the direction of American culture; but while the rhetoric was strong, the people were gracious. Rudy Giuliani, whom many attendees had vowed not to vote for if nominated, was greeted warmly and treated respectfully.

And yet, the benign zeal with which social conservatives approach their politics is distinct in the political landscape. And no wonder. Many of the issues that traditional social conservatives care about most, namely abortion and other bioethical issues, are matters (literally) of life and death. This fact gives them an earnestness that those who are oriented toward fiscal conservatism and "defense conservatism" will never have, except in times of depression and war. Moreover, while the arguments for these positions are mostly secular in nature, the energy is frequently grounded in a religious commitment to defend the rights and freedoms of all people—especially those who cannot speak for or defend themselves. In this way, many social conservatives view themselves as standing firmly within the political tradition of William Wilberforce and Martin Luther King, both of whom made secular arguments while inciting and utilizing religious zeal.

These sentiments were on full display at the Values Voter Summit, but the relative absence of people my age was startling. While my friends are all avowedly pro-life, we wear it differently than our parents. We worry about the ethics of war the way our parents worry about the ethics of stem cells. Our concerns with immigration are about the protection and preservation of human rights, not the preservation and protection of the American borders and culture. This diffusion of interests has led to a shift in sentiments—we are more excited about working to end human rights abuses in China and elsewhere than about ending abortion in America.

These shifts are, I suspect, largely the result of a weakened sense of nationalism due to the recent economic boom. People my age have never lived through a serious recession, which allowed many of my most advantaged and involved peers to travel and study abroad, often giving them a sense of guilt about the pleasures they had access to at home. This was particularly true of my evangelical community of friends with whom I grew up. The increase in mobility and in global communications shortened the distance between America and other nations, weakening the fervency I was given by my parents for American nationalism (and capitalism).

But both my parents' generation and my own share a deep skepticism of the politicians who seek to win our votes. Because we think the stakes are crucial, social conservatives want to know that the candidates we elect really will include our issues in their platforms and goals. This cynicism is particularly rampant among my friends, the majority of whom are so jaded by overexposure to the media that they expect to be used. This places a premium on the public persona of the candidate. Thus, for most of my friends, the appearance of being "authentic" was more important than the candidate's actual policy positions. We want to know whether our leaders are the "real deal," or whether they are simply pandering to us to win our votes—as Jimmy Carter, the first to tap into the evangelical voting bloc, did back in 1976.

The Values Voter Summit of 2007 embodied many of these themes. Two candidates, Mike Huckabee and Mitt Romney, both needed to win over social conservatives to clinch the nomination, and their respective failure and success were both determined by their performance there. While Romney eventually won the straw poll, he took a step backward in the race as social conservatives—of all ages—rallied around Huckabee and made him a serious contender for the nomination.

Mitt Romney's relationship with social conservatives is extremely complex. The most prominent question during the primary season was whether his Mormon faith would prevent evangelicals from voting for him. For most of us younger conservatives, this wasn't an issue. We understand the "separation of church and state" and don't tend to evaluate candidates based on their religion (which is why Republican attacks on Obama's religious ties fell flat).

But Romney's campaign had other problems. For one, he was quickly labeled a political opportunist and unfavorably compared to another wealthy Northeastern politician with good hair, John Kerry. There is some legitimacy in this complaint. No one doubted Romney was economically conservative and was genuine in his distaste for governmental intervention in the business world. But his thin voting record on issues dear to the social conservative's heart, and some of his statements about his positions, made social conservatives worry they were about to be used once again as political pawns. Because social conservatives and young people tend to be cynical about politicians, the charge of being a "flip-flopper" is a death knell, as it means the person cannot be trusted.

Not only that, Romney failed in the early parts of the campaign to reveal the warm, humorous, and genuine side that I am told comes out in person. Many of my friends would remark that he seemed stiff and wooden. Such remarks were almost always qualified by an acknowledgment that this clearly wasn't that important, but the fact that it was a recurring theme suggests that Romney's own demeanor was more a liability than a benefit with millennials.

These complaints are deeper than simply Romney's public persona. Revealingly, Romney's support for torture was extremely distasteful to many young social conservatives. His attempt to unite the "three legs" of the conservative stool—strong defense, fiscal responsibility, and social conservatism—was sound enough, but it was too easily caricatured as support for big business and big military, which doesn't resonate with younger social conservatives who worry as much about the ethics of business and war as they do about sexual ethics.

Despite these problems, I went to the Values Voter Summit *wanting* to be convinced that Romney cared about our issues. After all, he had the political machinery and the money to win the election. But his performance and behavior only further reinforced our suspicion that Mitt Romney the politician was a machine who operated solely on the basis of political calculations.

Romney's speech was standard fare for social conservatives. He hit, as we might expect, all the right notes and said all the right things. But he was the only candidate who bused in his own supporters specifically for his speech alone, and he had also clearly given them the applause points in advance. The end result was that those who were not his supporters heard a speech delivered not to them, but rather to the cameras and to those who would applaud on cue. While this is a relatively normal part of politics, it was a horrible misjudgment by the Romney camp.

Not only did the artificial applause interrupt his rhetorical rhythm and create a flat-sounding speech, it reinforced our suspicions that Romney wasn't interested in persuading the room so much as giving the appearance that he had done so. This, in turn, exacerbated my suspicion that he was driven not by conservative ideas but by a simple desire to win.

Second, while Romney won the straw poll, it was evident to everyone at the event that, like his applause, he had effectively bought the victory. Romney was clearly the most organized and efficient of the Republican candidates, but his political instincts were way off.

By the end of the summit, it was obvious that Romney wasn't the first choice for most social conservatives, and that their disappointment had nothing to do with his religion. Instead, it had everything to do with his failure to communicate his positions in a way they found believable.

As for Huckabee, he may have lost the straw poll, but he remarkably managed to win the hearts and minds of both younger and older social conservatives. His performance was the opposite of Romney's: he had no preplanned applause lines but had to stop when people spontaneously burst into applause. He was endearingly self-deprecating, mocking his own Baptist exceptionalism. He was passionate, especially about the issues that matter most to social conservatives—abortion, bioethics, marriage, and American exceptionalism. Above all, he deployed the authenticity that Romney sorely lacked. It was evident that the audience trusted him, and he had a consistent, socially conservative record to back it up.

At the heart of Huckabee's speech was imagery and language drawn from Biblical themes. Yet it was not, as some portrayed it, a sermon. If anything, his use of Biblical imagery was firmly within the American rhetorical tradition. While increasingly uncommon, past presidents and candidates have often turned to the Bible for inspiration—and as a former pastor, Huckabee was clearly comfortable doing so. But his appeal wasn't one of religious identity, or an implicit shot at Romney's religious faith. Instead, Huckabee understood and fit within the odd fusion of religious fervor and political action that characterizes so many traditional social conservatives.

The response to Huckabee couldn't have been more different. The energy was palpable: it was Huckabee's room, and from that point on, social conservatives of all ages rallied behind him. What's more, though he lost the straw poll, it was a much narrower victory than anyone had expected, and the media narrative was dominated by Huckabee's performance and narrow loss. Romney went from straw poll winner to Values Voter afterthought.

Huckabee's appeal worked on two levels. First, he clearly understood what makes traditional social conservatives tick, and deftly catered to them. For a demographic resolutely skeptical about being used by politicians, Huckabee forcefully and firmly persuaded them that he was a social conservative all the way down. But he also trumpeted a conservatism that included the whole spectrum of human life, from conception to death, and found a hungry audience in people my age. His positions on illegal immigration were distasteful to many traditional conservatives, but a benefit to my friends. Huckabee's broadening of the social conservative appeal was right in line with the younger generation's shifting interests.

What's more, while Romney understood that the media matters, Huckabee had a more intuitive grasp that the way to win over the media—and its cynical audience—is to appear genuine, straightforward, and honest. He was the only Republican candidate to host a question-and-answer time for media and bloggers at the Values Voter Summit, which I attended. While it was my first time seeing him in a more intimate, less friendly setting, I was impressed by his wit and candor, and by his direct and gracious rebuttal to Max Blumenthal's attempt to make him look like an idiot. The same warmth and honesty that he presented on stage he displayed in person.

The rest of the campaign worked out largely according to this script—to both Romney's and Huckabee's detriment. Romney had the organization and the backing of the Republican establishment, while Huckabee continued to motivate his base with his rhetorical force. But Huckabee disappointingly failed to reach out beyond the social conservative base, while Romney never overcame the storyline that he couldn't be trusted on social conservative issues. In the end, they split the difference, and McCain ran up the middle.

In many ways, that weekend captured both the virtues and vices of the social conservative movement, including many of the tensions that younger people feel toward its senior members. Huckabee was eventually painted as a big-government liberal who was soft on national defense and foreign policy. And there's some justification for that, though not nearly as much as many Republican pundits thought. But because of that portrayal, traditional social conservative leaders dithered, refusing to rally behind Huckabee, even though the social conservative grassroots already had.

The bulk of my friends either went for Huckabee or Ron Paul—neither of whom were sanctioned by the Republican establishment or by the traditional social conservative leadership. While Paul's supporters are largely libertarians, Huckabee tends to attract those who are more comfortable with government intervention on social and economic issues—a sizable portion of people my age. This difference is partly why Romney's efforts at reassembling the "three legs" of the conservative stool didn't gain much traction with us. The military interventionism that Romney touted doesn't sit well with our libertarian impulses, and the economic libertarianism doesn't sit well with the broadened aims of a newer social conservatism.

This broadened social conservatism was key to Huckabee's appeal with younger voters. In many ways, his was the most recent iteration of "compassionate conservatism," which still has an audience—albeit tacitly—among many of my peers. Indeed, our distaste for George W. Bush was grounded in his tactical shift away from compassionate conservatism—and domestic policy in general—toward the war on terror. Huckabee, it seemed, was more similar to Bush in 2000—for better and worse.

What's more, it's clear from Barack Obama's election and Mike Huckabee's popularity with younger people that being "authentic" will do more for a candidate than either leadership experience or appropriate policy positions. The throwaway line from many of my friends that Romney seemed robotic was more than simply a qualification: it was, instead, the backdrop for their reservations about his trustworthiness. The only thing that could break through that cynicism is a strong sense of authenticity, humor, and warmth—all of which Huckabee had in spades.

Still, it wasn't easy supporting Huckabee in the primaries. He was rarely treated fairly or well by the Republican punditocracy, who largely failed to understand his gravitational pull for people my age. At the same time, his inability to expand his base beyond the social conservative segment was largely due to his failure to adapt his rhetoric to new audiences, a failure that made many of my friends uncomfortable. Young social conservatives remain suspicious of the sort of religious fervor that animates much of the traditional social conservative movement, and Huckabee's rhetoric clearly tapped into that stream. His use of Biblical imagery is better suited to previous generations of American political discourse, and his inability to communicate in other modes made it difficult to persuade non–social conservatives that he was really equipped for the job.

Those limitations partially explain the phenomenal appeal of the light that eclipsed him, Sarah Palin. Palin's personal narrative, ease, and authenticity all made her extremely likable to most Americans, and grounded our faith and trust in her. And for social conservatives, that's the preeminent virtue. But unlike Huckabee, Palin introduced the possibility of a conservative with traditional social values who knew how to articulate them without potentially offensive religious overtones or rhetoric. Palin's social conservatism as it was presented in the campaign (and thereafter) was grounded not in her religious beliefs as such, but in the reality of her family life and her decision as a mother to birth a child with Down syndrome. And that "personal testimony," while not explicitly religious, strikes a deep chord with social conservatives of all ages.

The Values Voter Summit of 2007 captured many of these dynamics. Our politics—of both generations—are largely determined by our implicit trust or lack thereof in our candidates. Neither my friends nor my parents play "identity politics"—instead, we care about honest representation, that the leaders we elect will not betray us. But the positions we want represented are shifting, and the shape and direction of the social conservative movement needs to respond accordingly.

2

PURSUING HAPPINESS

Joseph Ashby

During our first year of marriage, both my wife and I attended college. My wife was twenty-three and had 30 credit hours remaining before graduating in sociology. At twenty-one, I began my first-ever college semester three weeks after we were married. I stood an unwieldy 153 credit hours away from a mechanical engineering degree.

Despite the heavy class loads that awaited us for years to come, we resolved not to let schooling keep us from starting a family. We were young to have kids, by today's standards, but we were old for our age. My wife had lived on her own in three countries, I in two. Whether we decided to have kids, start a business, or follow dreams of another sort wasn't what mattered most. We weren't some sort of tragic or heroic figures. It was what we chose, the life we wanted. To borrow a famous phrase, starting our family when we did was the path we took in "pursuit of happiness."

We knew that pursuit meant certain challenges. Primarily, we didn't have any money. As young as we were and with our education unfinished, the best jobs we could find were unskilled and entry-level. Subtracted from our meager earning capacity was the time we dedicated to our university studies.

Despite the challenges, we believed that we could do it. We set out with the romantic idea that with our resourcefulness and work ethic, fueled by the love we had for each other and for the family we would raise, we could construct a life worth living.

In retrospect, it seems almost clichéd, like something from a lazily written nineteenth-century novel based on the out-of-fashion idea of rugged individualism. But our life was real. Certainly the bills in the mail were real. The demands by professors and employers were real. In some ways, our lives could have fit into such a novel, except that I soon discovered that we lived in a more complicated century, and in an America less free.

I worked for a small lawn-care and landscaping company. We mowed lawns at homes, churches, industrial outfits, and some local baseball fields. From time to time, we partnered with a local homebuilder to provide the sprinkler, sod, and shrub installation for their new residential builds.

My wife worked in customer service, answering phones, e-mails, and online chats. The job was with a small local company that provided credit card processing for representatives of direct-sale companies. Her natural kindness and patience served her well while she spent day after day explaining to unwilling Mary Kay ladies how to use a computer to charge a credit card.

The money we earned during that year was more than just paying the monthly bills. We actually made more than we needed to live on. We put in the extra hours because we knew we had precious few months to benefit from two full-time incomes. Our plan was simple: put in the heavy work hours while we could, pay off the car, set aside money for the pending baby, and save as much as we could after that.

Each aspect of the plan was important. The most urgent part was cash for doctor and hospital bills. The most nagging part was the car. The savings would have the biggest long-term impact. We knew once the baby arrived, and as our coursework became more difficult, we would earn less. Setting aside money for the leaner years of college could be the difference between making it and not.

For the plan to work, we couldn't just earn money, we had to spend it carefully. We moved into a studio apartment, chose a cut-rate landline over cell phones, and found other ways to hold down our expenses.

One day, after coming home from work, I carefully crept through the living/bedroom on the way to the shower, cautious not to jar the grass clippings loose from my clothes. In the bathroom, I was surprised to find my wife kneeling at the tub, scrubbing and sloshing several pairs of pants. I asked her what she was doing. She explained that doing some of our dirty laundry in the bathtub helped her stretch out the time between Laundromat runs.

As we knelt side-by-side on that and other occasions, we couldn't help but chuckle at the simplicity in which we lived. It helped us appreciate what we did have. "You know," I used to say, "we may do laundry in our bathtub, but in many ways, we live better than the emperors of history." Kristin usually just smiled, knowing I was giving us both a pep talk. The encouragement worked, because it was basically true. No other people in history—or most in the world at the time—had so many material blessings. We traveled in the speed and comfort of cars. The best entertainment in the world was available at the local dollar movie theater. We could even control the temperature in our home. During those times on our knees at the bathtub, we tried to remember that in many ways not even Egypt's pharaohs or Rome's caesars had it as good.

Regardless of what amenities we could or couldn't afford, our focus was on each other and the baby we were preparing to care for. So even though we often concentrated on earning and saving dollars, it wasn't about money—at least not in any sense that I had ever thought of money before.

I began to think of money in terms of the decisions I made and their alternatives. Never before did life present so many difficult choices. How much studying was enough? How much work would be enough? In truth, there would never really be enough time for either, and yet we had to figure out how to do both. Most important, our young marriage also needed cultivation.

At times, the relentless demands of our schedules forced us to look at other options. We had enough money for our current needs. School deadlines seemed so much more urgent than earning money for bills that wouldn't arrive for months or even years. Spending time with Kristin was far more appealing than long Saturdays of lawn-mowing. Working less seemed so much easier.

But the dollars-and-cents reality of our situation meant that letting up was giving up. We had too many bills (tuition, books, rent, etc.) to expect that we could pay them without a wholehearted commitment to the plans we had made.

★ ★ ★

We achieved most of our goals. By the time our little girl, Isabel, was born, we had the money to pay hospital and doctor bills and owned our car outright. We even did well enough in school to get a little bit of scholarship money based on grades. But we weren't able to build much reserve cash. I didn't give much thought to our savings at the time. I supposed we didn't quite make enough or spent too much. We knew that accumulating money on top of paying for the car and baby was going to be difficult. Dollars can only stretch so far.

A few months went by. Kristin went back to work for about ten–fifteen hours per week. I kept my work hours in the upper thirties and started a new semester of school. We moved into what seemed like a palatial two-bedroom basement apartment. We had our new daughter to keep us company. (We thought the preparation for her arrival was exhausting, but she taught us what sleepy really meant.) Before long, she was sleeping more regularly, smiling at us, and lighting up our lives in a million different ways.

Tax time soon arrived. Our W-2s came in the mail. We determined which tax forms we should use and picked them up, along with their corresponding instructions, at our local library. Since we had few write-offs and didn't itemize our deductions, preparing our return was simple.

Once we completed our 1040 form, we wished it were more complicated, at least if that meant the taxes turned out differently. We reworked the numbers over and over, hoping to find a mistake. (We felt like something had to be wrong.) Our tax liability (mostly payroll) was more than we had paid in rent over the entire year.

I stared vacantly at the forms, as if to look right through the numbers. I thought about our grand plans and all we did to try and make them a reality. I remembered Kristin, who week after week put in forty or more hours of work. As her pregnancy progressed—as it happens with many expectant mothers—sleep began to be elusive and headaches and backaches became more persistent and severe. She fought through it. Her final full workweek ended just a few hours before she went into labor.

I remembered the times that year when, to push just a little bit harder, I worked until dark, after the rest of the crew went home. My lifeless arms were blackened with drying mud from sod slabs I laid down throughout the afternoon. My knees and the heels of my palms were raw from working on all fours. While dusk provided welcome relief from the day's relentless heat, it was a reminder of just how short some days seemed to be. Even as I loaded up the truck to stop work for the day, hours of homework and studying remained before I could lay my worn-out frame in bed.

We put our sincerest efforts into earning that money. The anemic balance in our bank account took on a new meaning. It wasn't simply a matter of earning too little or spending too much. The savings we worked to accumulate were sitting on Line 4 of our W-2s. We took some consolation in knowing we had actually earned the money. Unfortunately, we couldn't pay tuition bills with consolation.

That time in our life acted as a catalyst for me, not just personally but politically. When I was growing up, my parents were civically active, so I was somewhat aware of politics. But my interest level intensified when I had my own family to care for. The suddenly debilitating weight of government forced me to engage in ways I hadn't before.

Over the next few years, I set out to answer certain fundamental questions about government. Our experiences needed context, not just because they were so important to me and Kristin, but because they could be the experiences of anyone. While the specifics of each person's goals were bound to be different from ours, we were alike in that we all sought to make a life for ourselves.

To understand the events of our first year together, I had to clear away the muck of modern political convention. A story like ours was ideal fodder for politicians. The young couple, working while struggling through college as they prepare for their first child, scarcely able to make ends meet. It was the kind of human-interest tale that landed people in the gallery at a State of the Union address.

Situations like ours were politically useful because they engendered so much sympathy. Even we felt sorry for ourselves, for a time. During our brooding, we grumbled that people in a situation as difficult as ours should get a break. But the fact that we were sympathetic characters should not have entitled us to special treatment. We had no right to demand special benefits where doing so imposed injustice upon others.

Unfortunately, most political solutions were based on the favored treatment of one citizen over another. Policies such as increased grants for college students or hosts of other subsidies put a premium on certain kinds of people (usually those who invoked political sympathy). I knew that was a line of thought I could not endorse.

I had to go further back in time. I needed to look at the world outside the perspective of one year's tax return or a two-, four- or six-year election cycle. I analyzed the ideas of several influential philosophers, politicians, and authors. Of all the variations, details, and emphases of the various thinkers I studied, two principal worldviews emerged in every case.

According to the first philosophy, a just society could only exist if its members had the right to do what they wished with what they earned. The second philosophy dictated that for a just society to exist, some of what people earned must be taken so that all could bc maintained in relative economic equality.

The second vision was more in line with the political answers I found so hollow. Our circumstances exposed the logistical impossibilities of trying to guarantee minimum benefits for 300 million people. A centrally administered redistributive tax system could never know us or our plans well enough to do less harm than good over the long term. We were forced to pay thousands of dollars in taxes instead of making provisions for our difficult financial future. A social safety net designed to give personal aid could scarcely have been more impersonal.

Once the taxes were collected, we faced the demoralizing option of returning to the government to beg for the money back through Pell Grants, Earned Income Credit, food stamps, Medicaid, or other programs. Our sustenance and prosperity were delinked from our own faculties and efforts and tied to a bureaucrat's actuarial table. The system, meant to be humane, disregarded the very qualities that defined us as humans.

Besides the detached, bureaucratic nature of government taxes and payouts, there remained the weightier matter of freedom. I heard arguments that the bevy of federal safety net programs made Americans more free. As Franklin D. Roosevelt put it, "We have come to a clear realization of the fact that true individual freedom cannot exist without economic security and independence. 'Necessitous men are not free men.'"

President Roosevelt's archetypal statement begged what to me was a very profound question: at what cost would this economic freedom be purchased?

Put simply, for the government to ensure economic security it had to collect and redistribute taxes. But what precisely were taxes? In the tumult of political rhetoric about the necessity of aiding one group or another, many had lost sight of what it was that the IRS really does. The events early in our marriage provided me a powerful lesson in what the government was taking.

The health of our bank account, the balance of our car loan, and our readiness to pay doctor and hospital bills were external indicators that answered core questions about who we were. It is true that we were just working jobs and paying bills, but the routineness of it all shouldn't distract from its larger significance. It was in our daily tasks, which often left us physically and mentally spent, where we found out the depth of our dedication, love, and perseverance. The money we earned wasn't just ours, it was *us*, an extension of who we were no less than fingers are an extension of a hand.

The vision described by President Roosevelt relied upon taking the sweat of one man's brow and giving it to another as his own. Cries of necessity merely served as a smokescreen, covering up the true nature of a redistributive system. Certainly clothing was a necessity for the inhabitants of England and America in the early and mid-nineteenth century. But that necessity was no justification for the means whereby cotton was produced at such low prices in the Antebellum South.

Roosevelt's brand of freedom could only exist by subjugating one citizen to another—hardly freedom's ideal. This dichotomy was not new. Abraham Lincoln summarized the two views this way:

"We all declare for liberty; but in using the same word we do not all mean the same thing. With some the word liberty may mean for each man to do as he pleases with himself, and the product of his labor; while with others, the same word may mean for some men to do as they please with other men, and the product of other men's labor. Here are two, not only different, but incompatible things."

After I experienced men doing as they pleased with what we had worked so hard to earn, it was clear to me which vision embodied freedom and which was built on a lie. True justice was only possible in the society that protected the product of each person's labor.

In the end, we made it through college. We welcomed a second child during my senior year. Kristin continued her part-time work until I landed my first engineering job. My wage was high enough for us to live on and, with plans to add a third little one, we decided it was a good time for her to take a break from the labor force.

The experiences of our college years left a deep imprint on me. In many ways, I feel lucky to have had such a difficult ordeal. Had we been more personally prosperous or less intent on walking an uphill financial path, the realities of life and the difference between freedom and servitude might not have been so clear. As it happened, our life has spurred me to defend the right of all Americans to carve out their own lives, free from the repressive hand of government.

3

THE CONSERVATIVE GENE

Robin A. Dembroff

I should have pled the fifth. "Actually," I admitted, "I was homeschooled." Although at a casual party, I had somehow gotten myself completely entangled in a social policy debate. Two new acquaintances, also college students, disagreed with me over public school sex education: they supported the current system, and I contended that the curriculum should include abstinence education. The dialogue had been whirling along, each of us weighing the alternative view and responding (for the most part) with sensitivity and respect. That is, until a question was directed at me that, as if by default, derailed our conversation.

"Well, what did *your* school teach?" Following "I was homeschooled," my credibility dissolved faster than a California state surplus, not that such a thing would ever exist. Indictment bypassed trial: if I had been homeschooled, I probably had conservative parents, and so surely I grew up indoctrinated with Republican propaganda. Upon that logic, my opinion was flagged as the incurably biased but inevitable result of my upbringing. Our debate lost equilibrium, floundered like a drunken sailor, then capsized.

My peers, like poor psychoanalysts, reduced my opinion to the effects of supposed childhood trauma. I was annoyed. My roots had discredited me before, aborting many quality (and some slipshod) conversations about issues such as politics, economics, or ethics.

Not that I deny my upbringing has influenced my current views. Whose hasn't? My parents were and are bona fide conservatives: the type that will even tease themselves for so nearly resembling the middle-class conservative stereotype—they're only lacking something with a four-wheel drive. As their child, I'm without a doubt a cradle conservative of the Millennial Generation. Someone should make T-shirts.

I don't know a perfect definition of "cradle conservative," but I can offer some rough guidelines from my own experience. If a young, currently conservative adult was educated at home or a small religious school; had membership in Boy Scouts of America, Awana, or FFA (Future Farmers of America); and/or knew the name "Bob Dole" before conquering shoelaces, I would bet money he or she is a genuine, twenty-first-century cradle conservative.

My life certainly fits the bill. It is said some people are born with a silver spoon in their mouth; I was born with Rush Limbaugh in my ear. I have conservative Christian parents, grew up in a conservative Christian town, and now attend a conservative Christian university.

My sister, Ellen, and I were homeschooled for almost the entirety of K–12. During that time, we followed curriculum that included Bible and—oh, the scandal!—creation science. To my retrospective amusement, we studied these subjects in a room where a framed photograph of Ronald Reagan hung on the wall . . . when Reagan wasn't in office. Pro-life literature, *World* magazines, and Limbaugh's bestsellers stood prominently on the shelves, and I even recall enjoying a children's book titled *Ump's Fwat*, which I now realize was an allegorical lesson in the values of free-market capitalism.

I have memories of my mother crying when Clinton was elected (both times), and my father pessimistically swearing he'd "eat a playing card" if Gore did not win the 2000 election—which, to my indignation, he never did eat. Both of them seriously considered stocking up on canned goods and toilet paper when Obama clinched the presidency in 2008. After all, my dad pointed out, toilet paper might be worth its weight in gold if everything goes south. "Bona fide," indeed. Clearly, I'd be lying if I pretended my parents had nothing to do with my present-day opinions.

. . . Or my hometown, for that matter. My childhood mostly took place on two acres in Visalia, California—central city of Tulare County, where there are more churches than cars, more NRA members than churches, and more cows than all of them put together. In Visalia, hotels only reach maximum capacity during the annual World Ag (Agricultural) Expo, and the occasional tumbleweed or tractor might halt traffic at any time. Of course, Visalia has grown exponentially since my childhood, but I fondly imagine that the elementary schools still take field trips to dairies, and restless teens still go cow-tipping in night's smallest hours.

Bluntly, Visalia was and mostly remains a conservative town. I know residents who think that any Californian south of Bakersfield is a Los Angeles liberal, and anyone north of Fresno is a Bay Area hippie. Not that Visalia is absolutely, 100 percent partisan, especially now, four years and forty thousand citizens since I lived there. But my childhood atmosphere didn't exactly present a wide variety of viewpoints, particularly since most locals I knew were homeschoolers, members of my church, or both. Even at the university I now attend, liberal opinions—though not uncommon—are not predominant. I probably could have maintained a cozy conservative bubble without too much effort.

As my reminiscing illustrates, my conservative opinions didn't come from adolescent rebellion. Nor did I, as my parents did, restructure my priorities in light of adult experiences and responsibilities. I accept the assessment that, in a sense, I *did* inherit my views. My objection starts when, as in the sex-education debate, the judgment goes to a place I find uninformed at best and even—dare I say it—*intolerant*. There, discovering someone was "born" conservative spirals into unwarranted condescension.

What causes the spiral? It could be a purposeful attempt to resolve contradiction between believing conservatism is ignorant and recognizing, "Hm, this conservative doesn't seem ignorant." More likely, it comes from a fatalistic idea that childhood determines who we are as adults beyond mere influence.

When I was younger, I despised being "Ellen's little sister." I would either pretend not to hear or coldly reply, "My name is *Robin*." Of course, I was being a twit, but the situation is analogous to a cradle conservative's predicament: individuality was stripped away and replaced with association.

Risking the ire of sociologists, I will go ahead and call that *marginalization*. As with racial or gender discriminations, "born" conservatives are routinely jeered off the dialectical field—especially by peers, and especially in academic settings. Anyone with the alleged "conservative gene" should not expect to win any popularity contests. (I certainly never have, although I'd guess other factors played into that.) Ideological rebellion is more respected than agreeing with childhood authorities. No one mentions that ideological rebellion is just another breed of conformity. Instead, it's presupposed that beliefs would be acceptable if they come from media, peers, or academicians, but they are worthless if shaped by family, church, or a conservative education.

The logic is inconsistent and, at times, incoherent. I recall conversing with a classmate at Visalia's community college about whether or not marijuana should be legalized. Even though I had no firm loyalties, I played devil's advocate by taking the side that marijuana should remain illegal. The debate was not of highest caliber. My classmate's opinion was, to put it kindly, more personal than analytical. Following a slew of half-hearted objections, his main argument bubbled to the surface. "If I want to smoke pot, that's my business," he said. Then, changing tactics, he played the "buddy-buddy card." "You know what I'm talking about—you wouldn't want cops crashing your parties."

I admitted that I actually didn't care much. I'd never thrown or been to the kind of parties he was talking about. Shocked, he demanded, "But you've smoked, right? There's no way you got through high school without trying pot."

I tried to dodge the question with an enigmatic response—like it or not, being drug-free is not and never has been "cool." "I'm still in high school," I said. Meeting a look of bewilderment, I braced myself and clarified: "I'm homeschooled—I'm taking community college classes for high school credit."

His tone had been tight and defensive, nearing an exasperated squeak. It instantly relaxed. "*Oh.*" In that one sound echoed a lengthy verdict: "Well, it all makes sense now . . . you're *homeschooled*. You don't know how things really are, and you probably parrot anything your parents tell you." Of course. Clearly, homeschooling should disqualify my opinion about marijuana's legality—not. But what could I say? There was no defense against his garbled logic. Reason doesn't affect the unreasonable—I've learned that firsthand.

A particularly "educational" incident occurred during my involvement with pro-life activism. While we were demonstrating at the same community college, there was a confrontation between a demonstrator and a male student. The student told the demonstrator, also a male, "Who are you to talk about [abortion]? You'll never have to have a baby." Listening in, I asked him whether I, being a woman, was allowed to talk about the issue. His reply caught me off guard: "Have you ever had sex?"

"Uh, no," I replied, perturbed.

He pressed the issue: "Why?" Rapidly disliking the conversation, I replied that, if he must know, for religious reasons, but what did that have to do with anything anyway? Wrong answer, apparently. "Well," he snapped, "after you've been a single mother on the streets, you can come back with your right-wing religious trash." I stood, temporarily stunned by his deduction, unsure how to respond. He was obviously grasping for any reason to condemn pro-life beliefs, but—and this was most shocking—nearby students were being compelled by his emotional appeals. After he left, similar objections continued to be raised. There was always some justification for censure: squint hard enough, and eventually anyone will look fuzzy.

How ironic. Conservatives are continually slapped with the "intolerant" label, but trampling someone's views under the pretext that they fall short of arbitrary personal criteria well-nigh defines the term. Also, no matter how well-masked the wound, this intolerance moves beyond irony into injury. It is incredibly disheartening when an engaging discussion is dismantled, and worse still when it was insightful.

That was another lesson I learned the hard way. Last October, while in a Peet's coffee shop near University of California, Irvine, I saw that the student next to me was reading Plato's *Republic* dialogue. I itched to strike up a conversation with him, having recently finished it myself, and because I'm one of those nerds—everyone knows one—who can get excited about 2,400-year-old books. After sitting in indecision for a length of time I won't admit, pretending to be completely engrossed in a novel I won't name, and wondering about Irvine's protocol for unsolicited conversation, I finally piped up. "Do you like it?" I asked.

Suave like Hillary Clinton in a temper.

"Excuse me?" I'm pretty sure I scared him. Realizing I had to display my utter nerddom or sound flirtatious, I chose the less disastrous option. "*The Republic*. Do you like it so far?" He seemed relieved; I was awkward, but at least not awkwardly licentious.

As it turned out, he was a graduate student at UC Irvine, examining the political role of religion in Plato's hypothetical city. Intrigued, I questioned him further about his research. Our conversation quickly hit upon the root issue, separation of church and state, and we bantered back and forth. He made strong arguments for their complete divorce, and I countered with examples of mild but successful integration. Still on the subject twenty minutes later, he asked, "Be honest—would you report a professor for preaching in the middle of class?"

"Well," I smiled, "they'd be allowed to at my school. I'm not at UCI—I go to Biola."

Hello Foot, welcome to Mouth.

And sure enough. "*Biola?*" he asked incredulously, looking as though he'd suddenly noticed that I had two heads. "You mean the Christian school, right? Did your parents make you go there or something?" I attempted to explain my choice of university, but the damage was done.

His demeanor made clear that, so far as he was concerned, nothing but conservative indoctrination or insanity (same thing, right?) could possess me to attend "a right-wing Puritan institution." Our conversation devolved and, within five minutes, he announced that he "really should get going." I felt like I'd been dealt the "it's not you, it's me" line. When he left, I drowned my disappointment in the paperback, solemnly swearing for the umpteenth time not to get involved with strangers.

The experience isn't always so civilized, as I've especially discovered since taking up blogging. The Internet can have this peculiar effect wherein acting nasty doesn't seem so nasty. Hurling (too) honest opinions at disembodied text boxes doesn't require much bravery; it's like insulting a person behind their back. My encounters with electronic boorishness have mostly occurred while I was functioning as target practice for Left-wing "trolls"—blog-stalkers whose sole ambition is to tear down every article they read, beginning with ad hominem attacks and concluding with the dissection of comma usage.

My conservative background is clear from my profile, so I'm easy prey. Criticisms can be amusing: my favorite one remains an articulate assertion that I was "a retard from a retard school with retard professors." These charges aren't hard to laugh off—they are obviously absurd. At other times, though, I've been earnestly accused of everything from naïveté to bigotry, and all on the basis of my conservative education. This brings me to conclude that, if the Internet reveals unfiltered opinions, my beliefs are probably disregarded more frequently (and vehemently) than I'm told to my face.

Even talking to Republicans doesn't guarantee immunity. My classmate Andrew found this out while discussing politics with a childhood friend. His friend was a registered Republican who supported President Bush but planned to vote for Senator Obama, whom he considered more qualified than Senator McCain. Andrew, flabbergasted by his friend's assessment, listed evidence that spoke to the contrary. At this point, he was delivered a grave diagnosis: Andrew's upbringing had clearly infected him with bias and closed-mindedness.

Describing the event to me, Andrew said that his friend's reaction was as if "conservative childhood had forever negated [his] decision-making and logic capacities." As in Andrew's case, this condescension is usually from peers—difficult for young adults, who tend to seek their social group's acceptance. Sometimes the exchange of ideas is altogether avoided in order to escape being stigmatized.

A film student I know, Evangeline, confessed to having done exactly that while working as an intern last summer. It hadn't taken her long to discover that the movie studio listed heavily to the left. For example, she recalled that if the words "George Bush" were uttered, obscenities and groans would always follow. Because she was from a traditional home and conservative university, Evangeline expected her peers to disregard her opinions—perhaps even belittle them—so she evaded all political and religious conversations.

Any discrimination powerful enough to silence unspoken voices needs to be confronted. It's fallacious to assume that conservative nurture *determines* certain convictions. That would make sense if Right-wing parents could implant a "conservative chip" in their children—we can call it the RNC: Republican Naturalization Chip—but, in truth, every belief has an initial cause. Is someone's childhood education, or their parents, really an illegitimate origin of belief?

Say I start advocating private healthcare because a Magic 8-ball promised me that "you may rely on it." I shouldn't be hurt or surprised when no one takes me seriously. Even in that case, though, my opinion could be justified at a later time—maybe I become legitimately informed on the topic but still think private healthcare is the best option.

To redirect the analogy, suppose my parents used to lock me in a dingy chamber for hours and make me watch Republican propaganda. (I'm having a disturbing image of Sean Hannity wearing a monk habit and chanting "Small . . . Federal . . . Government.") As in the healthcare example, immediately dismissing any future conservative views would be unreasonable: they might have become well-founded.

If prejudice against cradle conservatives is rash in this imaginary, rather ridiculous scenario, the real marginalization is surely rash. Anyone pursuing personal conviction should eventually be *willing* to disagree with childhood authorities, but to think they *must* oppose them is reactionary. The beliefs of childhood are indiscriminate—they aren't necessarily false.

My opinions were unrefined at the age of nine. Nine-year-olds are expected to have unrefined opinions. In general, I blithely repeated what I'd heard from various sources, which could land me in hilarious scrapes, like the time I announced at a dinner party that Bill Clinton might be the Antichrist. Ten years later, I'm fairly certain I have better rationale behind my beliefs, even though the majority of them have remained static (don't worry, not the Clinton one). Despite that, my unaltered convictions are still dismissed as if they were the unthinking repetitions of a child, and certainly not informed or discriminating.

But if a belief were true, a discriminating person would maintain it. At what age is a person "discriminating" enough to—pardon the pun—conserve true childhood beliefs? For a native conservative, the reply seems to be "none, never." Maybe when I'm forty, I'll slip the stigma and be allowed to vote pro-life and dislike income tax. I won't be holding my breath.

Certain labels will probably always stick with me—I'm "Ellen's sister," have "father's nose," express "childhood's opinions." After a lot of fruitless angst, I've finally made a conditional peace with that. Provided I'm not less an individual because a sibling, or have less of a nose because of family resemblance, the labels are harmless . . . *maybe* even endearing. So when my beliefs aren't being disregarded because I was "born" into them, I'll willingly accept the title "cradle conservative." I don't regret being one. What's more, should I ever have children, *Ump's Fwat* will definitely be their favorite bedtime story.

4

SPLENDID ISOLATION

Michael Brendan Dougherty

First weeks of junior-year first period, 7:10 a.m. Me, with Brewster High School's soggy version of a sausage, egg, and cheese sandwich sitting on the corner of my desk. An orange juice carton in hand.

"Who here would support Prohibition?" asked Mr. Gallagher, our AP History teacher.

Unthinking, I shot up my hand, and was soon joined by three others out of twelve in our class. Juice dripped down my sleeve.

"This is surprising," said Mr. Gallagher. The eight potential gin-runners looked at us in disbelief. After all, history had rendered judgment. Prohibition didn't work, therefore the issue was closed.

"They're just being weird," one said.

I sipped my state-subsidized juice manfully. Something in me had changed. My impression from history as it had been taught to me was that one couldn't be a prohibitionist. Just as you couldn't believe in having a king of France after the bloody revolution, and you couldn't be laissez-faire after 1929.

Like many young people, I intuited that history had a direction. From the hut to the skyscraper, from superstition to reason. Friday, obviously better than Monday. My dim view was that politics, if they were meaningful, meant racing up the next plateau of human freedom and claiming moral victory over everyone else. Most important, don't be weird.

Awaking from such a view of history isn't all that unusual. Nor is it exclusive to conservatives. Most people can manage some sympathy for history's losers. Usually it's expressed as a bipartisanship of the past. "Ah, the anti-federalists were basically wrong, but they helped us get the Bill of Rights," or some such.

I never took Prohibition seriously. But my faked sympathy for one lost cause grew into actual enthusiasm for others. I looked through my grandfather's history books for the cranks that had made American politics churn. The Shaysites, Free Soilers, and Mugwumps. I learned that defeated ideas aren't dead, just down. Occasionally it falls to us to pick up their moldering banners, patch the chords, and carry forward.

In that time, between 1998 and 1999, there were two voices that mattered to me politically. On cable television, there was Madeleine Albright hissing at General Powell, "What's the point of having this superb military you're always talking about if we can't use it?" And (in one of my grandfather's history books) there was E. L. Godkin, founder of *The Nation* magazine, who wrote prophetically in 1896: "When we get our navy and send it round the world in search of imputations on our honor, we shall have launched the United States on that old sea of sin and sorrow and ruffianism on which mankind has tossed since the dawn of history."

Albright made it sound like American armed forces constituted some kind of tricked-out lawn mower, and she was anxious to ride it across Serbia. Faraway nationalist movements were a stinkweed in the global garden that Washington tended. Most Americans had never heard of Serbia or the Islamist-tinted Kosovo Liberation Army who were now our allies.

Months earlier, Albright's State Department had dropped the KLA from a list of terrorist groups and was pressuring France to do the same. This to save us the shame of where our zeal for human rights was leading us. If this was statesmanship, I was against it. I was embarrassed by it. In short, I was a budding isolationist.

This seemingly discredited impulse was the beginning and source of my conservatism, even as it alienates me from most conservatives today. The I-word is normally a pejorative, but I happily embrace it. The policy of isolation is simply this: America should avoid the quarrels of foreign nations. America's independence is worth guarding. It is not pacifism, though, of course, it recognizes that peace is a rare good and war a dangerous, unmasterable evil.

I wasn't alone among conservatives at that time. Even some of the most popular and conventional pundits echoed my own thoughts. Consider Sean Hannity, who asked in March of 1999, "Why should one U.S. airman give up his life when our national security is not in imminent danger?" On *The O'Reilly Factor*, Hannity went on to acknowledge:

"Slobodan Milošević is a bad guy. He's an evil man. Horrible things are happening. I agree with that. Is Bill O'Reilly then saying we go to Rwanda, Burundi, Somalia, Sudan? Where does this stop? . . . What this man is doing with ethnic cleansing is abhorrent, but sheer numbers—two thousand killed in the last year versus hundreds of thousands, millions in some cases, in other parts of the world. Are you saying the United States should go to all those places?"

My heart replied, "Hell no!"

Though the jingoes think it some kind of a slur against America's exceptional munitions, isolationism is the policy that takes seriously the great gifts of America: our geographic remoteness from the conflicts of Europe (and the Middle East), our friendly relations with our neighbors, and our great natural resources. Above all, it knows the limits of our power. It acknowledges, along with the moralizing neoconservatives, that there is evil in the world, but finds it wiser not to enmesh ourselves in trying to stamp it out. You have one "splendid little war" in the Caribbean and soon you're in an agonizing and dishonorable one in Asia.

Because isolationism grows out of America's natural advantages, it has found champions in every age. Habitually, conservative peacemongers cite Washington's Farewell Address with its warnings about "inveterate antipathies against particular nations and passionate attachments for others." These arguments came at a time when the American continent was still a playground for great European powers. Americans then routinely condemned the intrigues and permanent interests of Continental politicking; they were "blame foreigners first" isolationists.

The same leave-well-enough-alone impulse animated the Anti-Imperialist Leaguers who opposed President McKinley's ambitions in the Philippines. McKinley wanted to "uplift and Christianize" the natives, oblivious to the fact that the Jesuits had beat him by a few centuries. Rather than allow the Filipinos to choose their own leaders, McKinley pressed on. According to historian Paul Kramer, "U.S. officials predicted easy victories, underestimated guerrilla forces and, arrogantly assuming their objectives were universally shared, were shocked when U.S. troops were not greeted as 'liberators.'" Has a familiar ring. Five thousand American boys died in the muck. Over two hundred thousand Filipinos did the same.

Throughout our history, when the world-beaters say "Pack your little kit, show your grit, do your bit," and "we won't be back till it's over over there," the noninterventionists of the Left and Right have reminded us that some won't be back at all. So count the cost. Going over there changes the way we do things here.

The partisans of Little America aren't just hayseeds and hippies. America's belletrists from Ralph Waldo Emerson and Mark Twain to James Russell Lowell and William Vaughn Moody thought militarism a danger to the republic. Even the America Firsters of the 1930s, maligned as parochial Midwesterners or closeted anti-Semites, counted Kurt Vonnegut, Edmund Wilson, e. e. cummings, and Sinclair Lewis as members or symps. And not just liberals. Felix Morley, Henry Regnery, and John Flynn, conservatives before the movement, saw that war centralized government and uprooted its people.

I continued with my books and orange juice, while NATO's war against Serbian nationalists wound up speedily. The result was an Islamist-friendly Kosovo, and a Hague that bumbled through its humanitarian show trial of Slobodan Milošević for almost a decade.

Maybe I believed the so-called "peace dividend" was coming. Maybe I believed that the military would give me self-discipline and structure (even conservatives treat the military like a social experiment). I suppose even isolationists contain multitudes. So I conditionally enlisted in the Marines the following year, surprising my JROTC instructors. But my misadventure wasn't to last.

My recruiter, West Virginia–bred and whiter than a hospital sheet, was seriously jazzed about my ASVAB scores. "You could be in intelligence," he told me. But he kept hinting that I shouldn't let Uncle Sam's doctors see my sneaks when I took my physical in Albany.

"My feet stink?"

"Not exactly."

A week later, I went up to Albany to be examined. When I got to the last step of my physical, I bent over with my just-issued Gideon New Testament in my left hand, my scrotum in my right, a cough in my throat.

"Goddamit!" the doctor shouted. "You wear orthotics!"

He had discovered the little secret I had with my recruiter. My feet require little inserts in my shoes.

I sighed. My ass could be shot off with Washington's A-OK. But replacement orthotics couldn't be ordered to whatever base or battlefield I might occupy. I was out.

I came home, got accepted to Bard College, and packed my bags. I was a Marine-rejected peacenik going to one of the most progressive schools in the country during the Bush years and somehow I came out a conservative.

I didn't have some great reactionary revelation moment at Bard. Of course, I saw embarrassing sexual and political excesses. We had an "Alger Hiss Chair of Social Studies." And my first day featured an orientation course that introduced me to the free dental dams that we could use to perform "safe analingus." Typically crosswise. We were supposed to be subversively erotic but with a special fetish for emotional sensitivity and near-ritualized consent. To attribute all this to political liberalism is an injustice to unsupervised and well-fed youth.

But it was the contrast of my college life with the blue-collar work I did during the run-up to the Iraq War that sealed me as an isolationist and conservative.

I worked at a chemical factory in Danbury, Connecticut, with my girlfriend's father (now my father-in-law). Family-owned for generations, racially diverse in a way that Bard hoped to be, the company had roots. My fellow students pretended to believe in a dictatorship of the proletariat. My coworkers feared a dictatorship of liberal arts students, and gave me some good-natured grief about it.

They didn't want to command the means of production; they wanted a decent wage. I tried to imagine a dictatorship congenial to my floor-mate Robert, whom we called "Two Dogs." (So nicknamed because he was as ugly as two dogs making it.) He had a wild gray ponytail that swung as he barked at the ceiling. His disposition made him suitable for dirty jobs, nothing that required precision. A polity based upon his will would mandate beer-drinking during lunch breaks, and a Camaro in every garage.

I processed ammonium formate from 2002 until 2003. I still don't know what the stuff does. It came out of the mixers steaming hot and smelling like super-concentrated cat urine. By morning it was a frozen rock. After I sledgehammered the drums, stabbed it with a five-foot metal pick, and ran it through an industrial centrifuge, it came out the consistency of a snow cone. As I began to shovel it into its shipping package, I feared that in the heat-induced mania I would accidentally eat it and die.

My coworkers, goaded by the "Axis of Weasels" sensationalism of the *New York Post*, talked about turning Iraq into "a sheet of glass," and dropping a few on Chirac. Almost as if by osmosis they bought into the thinking that the war "would be a cakewalk." In every run-up our hearts authorize the perfect war. We throw a cloak of nobility over the very few casualties we expect and jump ahead to the ticker-tape in Times Square.

General Powell was making impressive presentations on WMD in Iraq. Bush was premising the inevitable invasion on UN resolutions. The pundits promised that liberal democracy would flower in the Middle East. Neoliberals castigated foot-draggers on the Left as unserious and insufficiently Trumanesque. Neoconservatives promoted Churchill.

Worse than their preening was that of the opposition. The most organized were Act Now to Stop War and End Racism (ANSWER), composed of World Workers Party members. For those of you who need a refresher on sectarian communists, the WWP distinguished itself in 1956 by supporting the Soviet invasion of Hungary. Armed democratists on one side of me, apologists for the Communist imperium on the other. Everyone had some hoary theory to export.

At night, after washing out the smell of snow-coned cat piddle, I turned to the stoic California poet, Robinson Jeffers (recommended to me by Justin Raimondo, the libertarian agitator at Antiwar.com). It was truly subversive stuff. When Jeffers's collection *The Double Axe* came out in 1948, one critic wrote, "In this truculent book, Robinson Jeffers . . . makes it clear that he feels the human race should be abolished." Another said that Jeffers offered "a violent, hateful book . . . a gospel of isolationism carried beyond geography, faith or hope."

Eagle Valor, Chicken Mind

Unhappy country, what wings you have! Even here,
Nothing important to protect, and ocean-far from the nearest enemy,
what a cloud

Of bombers amazes the coast mountain, what a hornet-swarm of fighters,
And day and night the guns practicing.
Unhappy, eagle wings and beak, chicken brain.
Weep (it is frequent in human affairs), weep for the terrible magnificence
    of the means,
The ridiculous incompetence of the reasons, the bloody and shabby
Pathos of the result.

As our troops rolled through to Baghdad, I hoped that I was wrong to be so pessimistic. I rejoiced watching happy Iraqis tearing down Saddam's statue and shaking their sandals at it. But those last three lines of Jeffers read like some forgotten prophecy. What had become of our great perorations about smart bombs and clean warfare, our fears about mass destruction, our propaganda about human shredders, and our hope for a democratic domino effect? The shabby pathos: thousands of dead Americans, a casus belied, and His Excellency Jalal Talbani shaking hands with Mahmoud Ahmadinejad.

Of course, the realities of war do much worse than disintegrate our wish for democracy on every atoll and sand dune. "We will come out of this war without a Constitution," bellowed John Randolph. If not the War of 1812 that he abhorred, certainly a future one. America's fever for Iraq's liberation produced predictable results: domestic spying, the Patriot Act, and authorized torture. You know, the eternal verities conservatives cherish. In heat for war, the right began defining treason down.

To break up my solitary readings of the isolationist Jeffers, my friends passed me an editorial in the *New York Sun* saying that war protesters were traitors, according to Article III of the Constitution. "There is no reason to doubt that the 'anti-war' protesters—we prefer to call them protesters against freeing Iraq—are giving, at the very least, comfort to Saddam Hussein," it read, before expressing hope that the NYPD would send two witnesses for each protester, "with an eye toward preserving at least the possibility of an eventual treason prosecution."

It could have been worse. During World War I, President Wilson called for "stern repression" of dissent. His vice president, Thomas R. Marshall, suggested that those "not in support of the Government" be stripped of their citizenship. Wilson dispatched volunteers, the "Four-minute Men" from the Committee on Public Information, to whip up hatred of Germany. The Espionage and Sedition Acts passed easily. It took a conservative Republican Warren G. Harding to finally free the Socialist war-dissenter Eugene Debs from political imprisonment.

Conservatives should be natural enemies of war. After all, war grows everything conservatives hate: the IRS, public debt, and, more generally, the scope and reach of government itself. That creepy stalker of the American dream, de Tocqueville, wrote: "All those who seek to destroy the liberties of a democratic nation ought to know that war is the surest and the shortest means to accomplish it." Conservatives are supposed to love the "near rather than the distant." War leads us to worry more about the textbooks in schools outside Qarbala than the ones our children carry. We empower Washington to rewrite history for Japanese schoolchildren. How can we expect it to leave Kansans or San Franciscans educating their own without supervision?

Bill Kauffman, a chronicler of the old and wild American Republic, points out that militarism also wrecks families. Divorce rates spike among uniformed personnel during wartime. "The images of families cleaved by the Iraq War and occupation should outrage family-values conservatives," he wrote in *Ain't My America*. I saw marriages bend and break under extended deployments in Iraq. And I've witnessed ill-advised marriages launched because of the promise of more generous benefits. Even children aren't spared the collateral damage.

When I was the child of a single working mother, conservatives gave the fictional character Murphy Brown grief for being a single working mother, a journalist. If only she wore combat boots. In November 2009, an Army cook named Alexis Hutchinson refused to report for duty in Afghanistan; she didn't want to leave her ten-month-old son. The twenty-one-year old single mother was arrested and nearly court-martialed; her son was placed in foster care temporarily. Eventually Hutchinson was demoted to private and discharged. Today, nearly 200,000 kids cycle through military-run day care called the "Total Army Family." Hillary Clinton was pilloried for saying "It takes a village to raise a child." Now it takes the Department of Defense.

I eventually migrated to the outskirts of the professional Right, as a staff writer for the *American Conservative*, a magazine that made room for isolationists, realists, and other castaways from the movement. It took a century to push what was the broad tradition of American foreign policy from the center to the edges. We elbowed our way to the margin of the great debates. But even now our small space seems cramped and perilous.

The fever for war will come again. Perhaps, one of our statesmen, not in mind to waste a crisis, will shout, "We're all Georgians now." This portends some shock advance not on Savannah but on South Ossetia. Or maybe we'll go sailing off to war for Taiwan, or South Korea. Every Pentagon promise is a tripwire.

The dissenters will be chased, first by the polemicists, maybe later by the police. We'll be dismissed "from the community of polite discourse" and accused by those mapping the bombing routes of wishing the annihilation of the human race. The spirit is as old and mad as Napoleon: Join or Die.

And there is only one answer: to hell with you! Who needs your subsidized salons? Leave me to the rusty chains and boiling cat piss; it's less rancid than your machine-gun idealism. You can have Madeleine Albright, Dick Cheney, and democratic peace theory. I'll take George Washington and the Jeffersonian radicals, the Mugwumps and Midwestern Main Streeters, the cranky poets and America First. Between these two great oceans, America can hold us all, from storefront Pentecostals to the Catholic bingo halls, from the skate parks of unsupervised youth to the literateers of Brooklyn. Let our glory dreams sparkle under Friday-night lights or in open-mic cafes. It's these that are worth defending. America is not some experiment, or a "progressive force" guiding the planet. It's not the judge of the principalities and powers. It's my home.

5

CHOOSING FREEDOM OR CHAINS

Andrew J. Foy Jr., MD

I have had many impassioned conversations with my medical colleagues over the past year, regarding the topic of health-care reform. It is not the fact that my beliefs are in direct opposition to Democratic reform efforts that causes controversy, but rather my opposition to the concept that health care is a human right.

I support this view by explaining my strong belief that the individual has the natural right to exist for his own sake, not as a means to society's ends. I believe the individual has the right to order his actions and possessions in the manner most consistent with pursuing his own happiness. I do not believe that one individual's need constitutes another individual's obligation to provide, but rather that it is the duty of free individuals to decide what and whose needs appear most important to them. I believe that problems in society are best solved when individuals act in a voluntary and spontaneous fashion and not through the coercive action of the state. I also believe the role of government should be strictly limited to its constitutional role of protecting individual freedom and securing peace.

As a follow-up to this explanation, I'm often asked some form of the following question: "What of the poor and those who can't provide certain necessities for themselves?" To this, I reply, "You won't be stopped from helping them."

If my reply comes across as heartless, it is not intended to be. In fact, it may even be looked upon as a challenge. In my experience, voluntarily providing medical services to those who can't otherwise attain them can be a highly effective form of delivering quality care. This is something I have come to recognize from my own experiences as a health-care provider. Upon entering medical school, I began volunteering for an organization that provided medical care to poor individuals living in homeless shelters throughout center-city Philadelphia. Not only was this activity highly satisfying to me on a personal level but it also played an important role in my development as a physician. Allow me to share some of my most valuable experiences and insights, which occurred while I've been offering my services over the past five years.

A typical night on the job would involve a group of medical students and a few residents piling into a van and making the short trip to one of our area shelters. When we arrived, there would usually be a small group of people waiting to sign up for appointments—these were the people who *really* needed to see a doctor. Nevertheless, once word spread through the facility that "the docs were in," a much larger crowd would gather for a chance to get shower shoes, soap, lotion, and reading glasses. When I first started working with this organization, I used to wonder where all the shower shoes and reading glasses went from one week to the next. The continued disappearance of these items led multiple inexperienced coordinators to devise schemes to track who had received shoes and glasses, with the intention of not giving them out to the same people over and over. Inevitably, after a few weeks, the no-longer-new coordinators would give up and things would go back to a first-come, first-serve basis. I've long since chalked it up to one of life's great mysteries—shower shoes and reading glasses just disappear. Period.

Besides the routine of giving out such useful items, we practiced real medicine. The majority of patients who came to us were seeking symptomatic relief for common complaints related to muscle strains, arthritis pain, the common cold, and allergies, which we typically treated with over-the-counter medications. Treating these conditions can be a very useful exercise for doctors-in-training. The ability to differentiate a common complaint from one that requires more urgent attention is a skill that every physician needs to develop. On multiple occasions, I've come across patients whose common colds turned out to be tuberculosis infections, pulmonary embolisms, infections of a heart valve, and heart-failure exacerbations. In making these more serious diagnoses, I learned to appreciate the importance of the clinical exam, as it was the only real tool at my immediate disposal. I've found the skill of physical examination to be personally invaluable at a time when classical medicine teaching and techniques are being deemphasized due to reliance on rapidly advancing imaging studies.

We also managed chronic diseases like diabetes and high blood pressure and, in my opinion, did the job superbly. Whenever possible, we would stick to the professional guidelines; however, there were times when we would run out of a certain drug. In those cases, we used our clinical judgment and selected the next best alternative. Some of our patients showed up every one or two weeks to have their blood pressure or blood sugar levels checked and their medications adjusted. I'm certain that our involvement with these individuals kept them well. I even developed long-term relationships with a few of these patients, who over the years have come to consider *me* their primary doctor. In terms of medical care, they know I can't provide them everything they might need but they also know I'll do everything I can to help them. Regardless of the environment, I believe this relationship is optimal and results in the best outcome for both doctor and patient.

One man in particular who stands out in my mind was an avid fisherman. Since this is a favorite pastime for me as well, I had no trouble bonding with him when I noticed he was carrying the Bass Pro Shop spring catalog. I had known this gentleman from previous visits as someone who was always polite and gracious. My previous encounters with him were short and to the point, and I had always given him anti-inflammatory medications for the arthritis pain in his knees. But on this particular night, we spoke about local fishing holes, our favorite lures, and exchanged big-fish stories. We agreed that smallmouth bass were the ultimate freshwater fish and that some fly fishermen can be real jerks. The next time I saw him, I gave him two of my favorite books, collections of fishing essays that just happened to be written by a liberal fly fisherman. Go figure.

As much as I enjoyed these exchanges, I could not help observing in them the ugly side of the welfare state. On first consideration, it could be easy to chalk these individuals' circumstances up to bad luck and lack of opportunity. However, more thorough inspection often revealed that many of these individuals were victims of their own poor choices. Many of them had continuing problems with drug and alcohol abuse. Many couldn't hold a steady job even though they had repeatedly been employed. My encounters with these individuals did not suggest they were unintelligent or without any useful skills. In fact, the opposite seemed to be true, which led me to ponder the question of why these people were in this particular situation. The answer was not the one I was expecting to find, or the one that I wanted to acknowledge, and it is no understatement to say that it fundamentally challenged my worldview. The answer was found in the simple words of my grandfather: "The government is the problem and handouts make people lazy."

Up to this point in my life, it would have been hard for me to characterize myself as particularly liberal or conservative. Rather, I thought of myself as pragmatic and, as such, above partisan thinking. I felt that societal problems could be solved if enough "smart" people—by that, I meant properly credentialed with the appropriate acronyms behind their names—came together on a solution and course of action. In fact, that is what I believed the role of government was: to solve society's problems. My grandfather, on the other hand, was not one of these "appropriately credentialed" people and, therefore, his views on such matters were closed-minded and not to be taken seriously. Or so I thought. After my experiences working with my patients, I could not continue to ignore his simple insights.

My grandfather's words are what professional sociologist Charles Murray calls "the popular wisdom." Murray states: "The popular wisdom is characterized by hostility toward welfare (it makes people lazy), toward lenient judges (they encourage crime) . . . The hostility one hears in the vox populi may account for the reluctance of many intellectuals to consider whether this view might not be right." Murray's work led him to conclude that there were three core premises of the "popular wisdom" that needed to be taken into account:

- People respond to incentives and disincentives.
- People are not inherently hardworking or moral. In the absence of countervailing influences, people will avoid work and be amoral.
- People must be held responsible for their actions. Whether they are responsible in some ultimate philosophical or biochemical sense cannot be the issue if society is to function.

Murray's pioneering book *Losing Ground* painstakingly provides the evidence supporting the "popular wisdom" that social entitlement programs have led to the deterioration of the very individuals and communities they were intended to help.

I witnessed this deterioration firsthand and it was disheartening, to say the least. The overwhelming majority of patients I encountered were receiving multiple forms of federal assistance, which were encouraging them to remain in their current situations rather than to take the steps necessary in order to "get off the dole." I have concluded that these individuals and their communities would ultimately be better off if these programs never existed.

Perhaps the worst side effect of these programs is the sense of victimhood and dependency they create among those who are receiving their benefits. I believe this occurs because the beneficiaries realize, after one or two failures to achieve success or independence, that it is much easier to fall back on government programs than to continue to work hard and struggle. To augment this problem, you have the professional politicians, usually Democrats, telling these individuals that the deck is stacked against them and they are most likely going to fail and therefore must vote for the party promising the most assistance.

This victimization mentality breeds an outlook on life that is almost certainly conducive to failure and dependency. How can a man be successful in life if he doesn't believe he has any shot to begin with? In my opinion, an individual with this outlook erects invisible barriers around himself, from which he cannot escape and therefore he inevitably gives up trying. When an individual indulges in the propensity to blame others or circumstances for his failures, I believe he only becomes disgruntled and ineffective.

This brings me to the central conflict in my argument against social entitlement programs. On the one hand, I acknowledge that there are individuals in genuine need of assistance; on the other hand, I also recognize that our social entitlement programs are forging chains in our society. These programs are bankrupting our country, they do not respect the rights of the individuals who must involuntarily subsidize them, and, most important, they *hurt* the very individuals they are intended to help by encouraging them to expect paternalistic support from the government. What is the solution then? I believe the answer is *you and me.*

As I mentioned above, I believe it is the duty and obligation of free individuals to decide what and whose needs appear most important to them. And I believe tremendous good can be achieved when free individuals act in a voluntary manner to help those who need a hand. These simple acts of kindness display the fundamental good that is in each of us. I believe that every individual has some unique gift that he or she can share with others; but unfortunately, I've noticed that many people do not contemplate how they can be of service, because they simply believe it is the government's role to perform those functions or because their capacity for kindness has been eroded by their lost sense of freedom, owing to the tremendous amount of involuntary income redistribution that already exists in support of the social welfare state. Moreover, the government cannot perform those functions as well as free individuals who intimately know the circumstances of those they are helping. To a government agency, the recipients are necessarily nameless and faceless.

My work offering medical care to those in need has absolutely proven to me that providing for people's medical needs is not as hard as the professional policy-makers would have us believe. Consider that the health-care bill, signed into law by the president in March of 2010 contains thousands of pages, along with hundreds of new government agencies, regulations, and new hoops to jump through for providers as well as patients. All of this will create unnecessary barriers between the patient and provider and decrease satisfaction for everyone involved. My medical colleagues, if they agree with nothing else I have written, will almost certainly agree with this last comment. Physician and patient satisfaction has declined precipitously with the growth of managed care—the specific result of prior government legislation aimed at providing for individuals' medical needs.

Voluntary service, on the other hand, erects none of these barriers. In fact, it serves the opposite purpose of tearing down barriers. There is no textbook known that can offer an individual the insights voluntary service can provide. These opportunities to connect with other human beings show us that we are more alike than different, that we can provide the services that others need, and that we can get back in return much more than we gave. This is such a simple concept, but no less profound. Voluntary service allows for personal connections rather than barriers to connections. It offers the opportunity for using our gifts and talents in a far more effective manner than we might have ever considered. It offers a framework for trust-building and the much-needed sense of gratification for both provider and beneficiary that become the building blocks for a successful relationship that is mutually advantageous. It offers the ultimate expression of individual freedom.

In my own field of medicine, I don't believe that the practice of individuals voluntarily providing services to those in need will create a medical utopia. Certainly it won't guarantee that every individual's needs will be met. But if history teaches us one thing, it is that collectivism's promises of equality and utopia have repeatedly met with failure.

We all want to make our communities a better place; the question is how. Instead of individuals advocating for the creation of more social entitlement programs like the recent health-care bill, which will not solve our country's health-care problems, they should go out (if they already aren't) and challenge themselves to connect and make a difference in the lives of people they can actually touch. In my opinion and personal experience, these human relationships will achieve a far greater degree of success and satisfaction than any government program ever will.

6

THE GIRLS I KNEW AT YALE

Nathan Harden

The joke goes like this: It's Halloween in New Haven, and two Yale girls are getting ready for the wildest party night of the year. The first girl is already dressed up and ready to go. Meanwhile, the second girl is still standing around in her bra and panties.

Yallette #1: We're gonna be late! Would you hurry up and get your freakin' costume on!
Yallette #2: What do you mean?

Every year, Halloween offers Yale students a chance to dedicate one night to the celebration of human vice. Whether it's booze, bongs, or booty pants, Halloween has it all—and in the extreme. At the end of the night, inebriation serves as an inhibition-lowering prelude to a campus full of random hook-ups.

Drunk sex is more the rule than the exception at Yale. I'm not sure which is scarier: witches and ghouls, or students with impaired judgment trying to practice safe sex. After six or eight cocktails, it's hard to tell the difference between a condom and a candy bar.

What always struck me about Halloween at Yale was the decidedly nonfeminist appearance of things. I remember occasional thematic events during other times of the year—such as the "Whores and Bankers" costume party—which seemed to run against the grain at an institution so famed for its liberal concern for women's rights. But Halloween was special. It seemed to bring out the whore in the general population, making so many girls memorable, not for what they wore but for what they didn't.

I wish I had a dollar for every prostitute outfit I came across on October 31.

One Halloween, I remember seeing a costumed streetwalker stumble across the quad in stilettos and a sequined miniskirt. It was irony in motion. She marched right past a monument designed by Maya Lin, called "The Women's Table," which commemorates the rise of women at the formerly all-male university. (Yale College was all-male until 1969.) The girl's bra was visible under a fishnet blouse—her own-me-for-an-hour appearance clashing with the idea of feminist empowerment that her presence at Yale was supposed to represent. Feminism got the girl to Yale, but apparently failed to provide her with any clothes for the journey.

At Yale, feminism carries on an oddly peaceful coexistence beside the hypersexualization and objectification of women.

The most visible feminist organization on campus is the Yale Women's Center. The Women's Center provides a host of health services to female students, such as sex education, free condoms, abortion referral services, and rape crisis counseling. The Women's Center also serves as a hotbed of feminist political activism.

During my years at Yale, I never once set foot inside the Women's Center. (I'm not even sure if my particular anatomy was allowed through the door.) But, through an improbable series of events, I became somewhat familiar with the sort of thinking that goes on inside.

In the fall of my junior year, I got into an acrimonious exchange on the pages of the *Yale Daily News* with a girl named Emily,* who was a student leader at the Yale Women's Center. She was known all around campus for her outspoken brand of hard-boiled feminism. Emily had published a crude opinion piece that dwelt at length on the sociological ramifications of the phallus and made copious use of the F-bomb. (The *Daily News* is not a family paper.) I responded with a letter to the editor that was, in hindsight, overly harsh. I think I congratulated her for "taking reflexive victimhood to unprecedented levels of vulgarity." That's how our friendship started.

Although our political views could hardly have been further apart, Emily and I soon found that we both shared an affinity for attention and controversy. I sent her an e-mail, apologizing for the harshness of my letter and commending her on the one point in her essay with which I did agree. We soon met in person.

Emily was a cute blonde and a promiscuous writer. She constantly besieged the student paper with articles and opinion pieces on various women's issues. She was fully committed to the boilerplate causes of radical feminism, including abortion, sexual liberation, and the propagation of various ethereal theories of gender. But what surprised me about Emily was that, while she was a feminist, she was also a hopeless romantic.

---

* Names have been changed for this essay.

Through her writings, our conversations about romantic life on campus, and countless video blogs on Facebook, I came to realize that, even though Emily was on the forefront of feminist activism at Yale, she was still pretty much like any other girl I had ever known. She wanted love.

Intellectually, Emily may have defended a lifestyle of casual sex. She used to send around e-mails inviting students to attend Yale's famous naked parties. (It's just what it sounds like.) But, emotionally, I could sense a hunger for something deeper.

Emily and I came from entirely different backgrounds. She grew up in Europe—the child of liberal American expatriates. I, on the other hand, was born the son of a Southern Baptist minister, and was twenty-one before my first trip abroad. At Yale, Emily was part of the mainstream liberal culture. I, on the other hand, attended Yale as one of a minority of moral outsiders. Consisting mostly of religious conservatives, this minority rejected the mainstream sexual culture of random hook-ups in favor of abstinence, moderation, or, at least, some sort of monogamy. In the context of Yale's "liberated" sexual culture, we prudes were the deviants.

While religious faith and moral convictions set me apart from the prevailing sexual culture, my personal history further distanced me from the world I inhabited. I came to Yale in my mid-twenties, having followed a circuitous route that included a two-year stint at a smaller liberal arts college as well as several years out working in the real world between high school and college.

My upbringing featured all the trappings of what liberals think of as the "repressive" religious right. Although my father was a Southern Baptist minister, he was the music director, not the pastor. For this reason, the house was always full of music, and I started taking piano lessons as soon as I could walk. Through music, I gained an instinct for the sensual and passionate side of life, in spite of the fact that I warmed the stiff church pews no fewer than three times a week.

Not that I was ignorant or, really, innocent. By the third grade, I had been fully awakened to the remarkable dimensions and possibilities of the female body. When I was growing up, there were always cousins or older neighborhood boys who somehow managed to get their hands on the magazines from the back of the rack at 7-Eleven.

If there is such a thing as an eight-year-old Casanova, I was on course to be that boy.

After my parents' divorce, however, my mother decided to home-school me. I skipped two grades in math but lost the opportunity to perpetuate the series of grade-school crushes I had cultivated since kindergarten. I never saw the inside of a public school again.

As a teenager, I was isolated from temptation. My small church provided few opportunities to meet girls; Boy Scouts none. In any case, I figured it was all for the best, since I was committed to a radical form of abstinence, eschewing not only sex but also petting, kissing, dating, and all forms of conspicuous flirting. (I often failed on this latter point.)

Instead of girlfriends, I had three sisters. I came to feel particularly protective toward the two younger ones. They helped forge my desire to act responsibly toward women. I learned that it is easier to treat women well if you remember how you want other men to treat your own sisters. In other words: Hands off, or else!

My parents' religious values eventually became my own. I left home on my eighteenth birthday and moved to Seattle. By then, my determination to save myself for marriage was firm, and it was something I viewed as a matter of religious devotion, as well as a gift to my future wife.

During the years in which most of my peers were amassing credits and cramming for exams, I drifted through a series of cities, jobs, and adventures. I spent a year tossing bags into the bellies of jumbo jets for United Airlines. Two years waiting tables and singing Sinatra standards in a Florida country club. I lived at sea for six months.

My parents thought college would be a waste of my time, and advised me to pursue my music career instead. (I had shoulder-length hair and three gigs per week by this time.) In any case, they figured most colleges were full of humanists and atheists and perverts. When I ended up at Yale, their pride in my achievement was tempered by reservations about the liberal education I was about to receive.

However valid their concerns might have been, by the time I made it to college, I had, in fact, done a lot more living than most of my Yale classmates. My views about sex, therefore, were not the views of a cloistered, easily corruptible homeschooler who had spent his life making his own clothes, churning butter, and fearing the outside world. They were the views of one who had seen what the world has to offer, and yet made purposeful and difficult moral choices about the proper use of his own body (as well as the bodies of any willing hot babes he happened to meet).

One might think that the radical abstinence of my upbringing, as well as my general lack of experience with women, would have rendered me shy and helpless around girls. But the Casanova of my childhood lived on. Maybe it was the lingering conceit of adolescence, maybe it was the guitar, but I moved with confidence around girls—a puritan on the outside, a lothario within. Abstinence is hard, but possible; I suppose I am living proof.

I forgot to mention the final and most important distinguishing fact of my personal history prior to Yale. I got married.

Fresh from my time at sea with a medical missionary organization, I moved to Nashville and fell dangerously in love with a young artist who seemed to encapsulate the dreams of a thousand celibate nights. We met, courted, and married in six months. Two weeks with her in Puerto Vallarta served as a prelude to my freshman year.

Christianity, marriage, and life experience all helped give me a unique perspective as I entered college at the age of twenty-two. I was close enough to my classmates in age to assimilate into college life, but far enough away to see it for what it was.

It did not surprise me that very few of my classmates shared my views about sex. What did surprise me was the degree to which sex on campus was separated from actual relationships. I soon learned that most undergrads saw sex as something a few steps beyond a hug—certainly no indication that two people were in a dating relationship. Sex in college exists apart from and, occasionally, as a prelude to love. Many girls engage in sex with the hope that it will lead to "something more."

At Yale, a guy shows up at a party and meets a new girl. They have a few drinks, nod to the music, ask each other, "What's your major?" and "What college are you from?" (At Yale, dorms are referred to as "residential colleges.") Maybe they dance. At this point, if the two are getting along, it is not considered unreasonable for the guy to expect oral sex at the end of the night.

Men, I would argue, do not benefit spiritually or morally from such a promiscuous culture. But women receive the worst end of the bargain. Indeed, polls indicate that more women than men are dissatisfied with their sexual experiences in college.

There is very little stigma out there for male sluts. (Have you ever even seen those two words side by side?) On the other hand, girls face constant pressure to put out. Yet if they do sleep around, they risk vicious stigma—especially from other girls.

I remember listening to a female classmate complain about a certain recognized feminist leader on campus, whom we'll call Lydia. Lydia had, according to my classmate, had sex with all my classmate's male friends. And if that weren't enough, Lydia also had sex with one of my classmate's female friends. However, the contempt in my gossipy classmate's voice could scarcely veil her jealousy.

At Yale, caring about love is a weakness. If a girl resists, doesn't get with the program and get into bed, another girl will take her place. Expectations are so slanted toward casual hook-ups that any girl who holds out for a meaningful relationship is in danger of being left out altogether. It's either "friends with benefits" or another Friday night spent alone. As a result, many girls go further and faster sexually than they really want to go.

Hypersexualization at Yale is, in part, a reflection of broader trends in our culture. It starts early. These days our junior high schools are full of girls who dress like Britney Spears and turn out favors like Monica Lewinsky—all in a desperate attempt to keep up with what our culture tells them will make them desirable. But there are many surprising cases in which the Yale administration itself is responsible for creating an environment that objectifies and demeans women.

If college kids are guilty of sexual excess, it's not all that surprising. But what about the folks with PhDs? I arrived at Yale with an initial sense of awe, strolling under Gothic archways, imagining a future full of lofty educational experiences. But I was soon struck by just how, well—sexy a Yale classroom could be.

On one occasion, a movie we watched in Spanish class contained girl-on-girl action. The professor showed us the film in order to teach us the Spanish language in an entertaining and engaging way. But, personally, I found it difficult to focus on grammar and syntax AND breasts and lesbian sex all at the same time. Later, a friend of mine described her similar experience of being shown a "porn" film in Portuguese class. When I complained to Yale's director of language studies about the lewd in-class material, she told me it was too difficult to find foreign-language films in which actors keep their clothes on. Learning a romance language at Yale is, consequently, a very erotic experience.

There were numerous other cases in which questionable films, or even good old-fashioned pornography, were shown under the official sanction of the university. I remember when the film studies department announced a series of Asian porn screenings during my junior year. Alas, at Yale, multiculturalism finds a comfortable home alongside moral relativism. Even the perverse is diverse.

I shouldn't fail to mention the X-rated sex-ed seminars. I once attended a classroom demonstration in which hundreds of students received instruction on how to use dildos, vibrators, and various arousal creams. We even received special advice on "anal play."

On another occasion, a porn producer was invited to campus. He provided expert commentary during the screening of his film—giving new meaning to the idea of intellectual stimulation.

All of these examples demonstrate that Yale has been fully co-opted by a radical culture of sexual excess. And the presence of university-sanctioned pornography shows that Yale's commitment to women's equality is mere lip service.

The presence of women on campus, along with various granite monuments to equality, give the appearance that Yale is a place where women are respected. But the porn and ribald sexuality emanating from Yale's classrooms send a very different message: that women at Yale are measured not by their achievements or character but by their suitability as objects of male desire. When young girls arrive as wide-eyed freshmen, they soon learn what is expected of them. During my first term at Yale, I captured the attention of a young female classmate, whose eyes lingered on me during class just long enough to signal her feelings. I knew her first name, Jessica, but little else about her. I am sure we had never had an actual conversation outside of class. You can imagine my surprise when, one day, this girl solicited my company for a weekend getaway. I was not in Momma's homeschool anymore; that much was certain.

For reasons religious, moral, and matrimonial, I could never have assented. But, of course, Jessica didn't know I was married. And that's just the point. We didn't know each other at all. In that moment, I felt embarrassed for her, for how easily she had offered herself. Her words shocked and enticed and saddened me all at the same time. Jessica was a beautiful girl, not one who had any trouble attracting male attention. She would easily have gained my hearty assent had I been a man of lesser morals and different circumstances. She clearly didn't know what she was worth.

So many girls I know at Yale seem caught between two personas: part pin-striped professional and part pasty-wearing pinup. These are not air-headed bimbos I'm talking about. These are seriously talented women, many of whom will go on to enjoy high-powered careers. Nevertheless, as Yale students, they are part of a culture in which both feminism and laissez-faire sexuality are widely embraced. But the two ideas don't really work together.

In a 2005 Harris poll, 58 percent of women agreed with the statement "Pornography is demeaning toward women." It is remarkable, therefore, that Yale—a university so well known for its political liberalism and so adamant about its commitment to women's rights—should demonstrate such ambivalence about the pornography that is displayed year after year in its own classrooms. To my knowledge, no feminist student or faculty member has ever challenged Yale's president, Richard Levin, on his willingness to turn a blind eye when professors or student groups use university resources to create a humiliating environment for women.

Yale is full of surface-level posturing on behalf of women. Meanwhile, under the surface, one finds nothing but limp, morally directionless obeisance to moral relativism and base sexuality.

Near the end of my senior year, I was sitting at the window of an ice cream shop, working on a cone of double chocolate trouble, when Emily passed by outside. She was crying. Our eyes met for a moment, then she turned away suddenly, looking horrified that I had seen her so broken. I didn't know what she was crying about. But I've seen a lot of girls cry, in my time, and I had a feeling that it had something to do with a guy. Regardless, I'll never forget her face. She reminded me that day that even the most strident feminists may harbor more delicate feelings within, and may have motives that are invisible—even, perhaps, to themselves.

It is easy for conservatives to make noise about moral relativism and cultural indecency. But we should never forget that there is a human corollary to all of the ideological arguments that fuel our culture wars. Ultimately, the well-being of countless individuals is at stake.

Today, one out of every four teenage girls in the United States has a sexually transmitted disease. Meanwhile, young girls navigate a youth culture in which sex is treated as a step toward a committed relationship, not the end result of it. Feminists are reluctant to face the failures of sexual liberation. But the tragic excess of the hook-up culture among American youth testifies against them.

The hypersexualization of young girls has left them powerless. Feminist leaders, by and large, have been too enamored with the sexual revolution to see that its actual effects have disempowered the women it was supposed to liberate. At Yale, I have seen the wreckage of feminism's sexual aftermath. The whore-as-empowered-woman motif has produced a generation of disaffected coeds. Many are my own friends.

Three of the last four presidents and several justices on the Supreme Court were educated at Yale. If you happen to visit on Halloween, and you see all the chem-majors-turned-prostitutes walking around, that's when such statistics become truly scary.

At Yale, young women are the special targets of a radical sexual culture, a culture enabled by the morally bankrupt brand of feminism propagated at our nation's leading universities. Yale is full of self-proclaimed feminists who are dedicated to upholding the inviolate autonomy of the female body. But their lingering devotion to 1960s-era sexual liberation has left them unable to see how the excessive sexual culture at Yale pressures girls into doing things with their "autonomous" bodies that some of them would rather not do, and which, statistically speaking, many will regret later on. Before you know it, these girls are leaning their autonomous, fishnet-cloaked bodies up against the visionary stone work of Maya Lin, looking like $20 might buy a good time for any passerby.

Again, I don't blame the girls so much as I blame the culture they are a part of. What can Yale do about all this sexual excess? I'm not sure, but canceling Asian porn night might be a good start.

All three of my sisters have gone to college, and one is yet to finish. They are responsible young women. Nevertheless, when I think of them trying to navigate the pressures and expectations of university life in these enlightened times, I am convinced of the need to expose the educational irresponsibility at Yale and elsewhere. Most of the girls I knew at Yale are, as I like to remember, someone else's sisters. When I think about Emily, Lydia, Jessica, or about any one of those Yale girls in Halloween hooker attire, I never forget that my own sisters could easily be in their shoes.

7

A NONCONFORMING RECONSTRUCTION

Justin Katz

With the cold granite of the exterior walls exposed from the inside and the modern conveniences of electricity and plumbing disconnected for the early phases of reconstruction, the wind gusted through closed century-old windows as if through the glass itself. Just near enough for me to see the froth, waves cascaded a chill across the rocky New England shoreline, and it tumbled as wind along the frosted hill and hardened a still, man-made pond.

Alone in the gutted basement, previously servants' quarters of an old Newport mansion, I'd pause in my carpentry from time to time to listen for the echoes of the long-laid hammers of the builders, whose marks were visible in the old lumber. They'd driven handmade nails into studs and subfloor boards by the thousand, and it seemed as if the rapping might yet be audible beneath the hum of the CD player cycling through Bach adagios and the scream of metal in wood as I pried the materials apart. In the rasp of my own breath, as I worked, I could hear my predecessors' saws scraping back and forth across the aromatic fir, cutting two-by-fours that were actually two-by-four.

When I needed fresh lumber, a cell phone and a truck would bring shipments to the job site, and although the numbers by which I described the boards' dimensions were the same, they were mere representations—at best, denoting the width and thickness that the rough-cut lengths had been before machines had planed them down, smooth and standardized, a half-inch lost in each direction.

Plane as we may, wood's a stubborn thing. Its twisting habits wreak quickly from within what the burden of external weight takes decades to accomplish, and often I found it more efficient to clean and reuse the materials that I'd inherited from those who'd compiled the structure before me.

Around the time when the workers who'd built the mansion were born, new notions of man's nature were being formed. "Whoso would be a man must be a nonconformist," wrote Ralph Waldo Emerson in "Self-reliance" (1841). The carpenters' fellow New Englander explained: "Infancy conforms to nobody: all conform to it, so that one babe commonly makes four or five out of the adults who prattle and play to it."

Through the plying of such memorable phrases, the likes of Mr. Emerson made individuality provable only by forcing others to stoop in order to communicate. Between the years that the mansion's foundation grew out of the waterfront ledge and the morning that I gazed through the rippled, sagging glass of its lower apertures, that principle spread as rot, with each generation striving to know less, culturally, than the previous. Transcendence beyond the need for strictures and forms had crumbled into a rejection of the very suggestion that one must understand convention in order to tweak it meaningfully.

Thus the peculiarity of our time is that one must, in essential philosophy, be conservative to be contrarian. The practice of my hands taught me to disassemble servants' quarters and build spacious apartments in their place; exercise of the mind brought discernment that Western culture had so thoroughly deconstructed itself as to risk lacking the materials to rebuild. To capture the individualist's liberty, one must give the past its due and understand that freedom comes from self-mastery, not—as Emerson averred—from "the nonchalance of boys who are sure of a dinner." Nonconformity for its own sake is just conformity for the sake of something else—a something that others are ever too anxious to supply.

I came to this conclusion through painful experience as a specialist in falling through cracks. A lifelong observer might be justified in claiming that I ran from one posture to another, rebelling against the entire culture one segment at a time. From an internal perspective, it felt more accurate that my differences discomfited inhabitants of every niche along the spectrum.

Born into a world dominated by the Me Generation and raised in a Northeastern culture contemptuous of the yuppie daydreams of the era, even as its every household pined for the markers of material success, I learned liberalism as a pose. The sixties and seventies provided a social script that the properly educated were compelled to follow. Out among the people, President Reagan was simultaneously acknowledged as the best man for the job and targeted as an appropriate subject for mockery. That was just the way it was supposed to work: revere by breaking down and break down that which others revere. Pop culture fed us the opinions that we were supposed to have, and I was disinclined to challenge them.

One could spin the fact as either a slight or a compliment, but I found myself especially susceptible to the confusions of the time. A classroom of girls advised me on the image that might transform me into a datable teen bachelor—sweaters from Britches in the North Jersey mall and pants from the Gap, hair cut in the soft-spiked style of the day—yet found me too risky to date themselves. The crowd of Different People with whom I shared an interest in music could not abide my preppy wardrobe. The contemporary crowd of Outsiders, conversant in cars and drugs, were embarrassed by my poor constitution for illicit substances, and the students with whom I shared the upper percentiles of academic achievement were unnerved by my lust for experimentation, which I pursued with the vague sense that the very next combination of attributes that I'd try would be the one to make sense of my life.

Adulthood taught the lesson that the personal becomes professional when at last one's dinner no longer arrives with the dependent's surety. After the disastrous discovery that I lacked the balance for the well-trodden progression from high school to college, I dropped out for a detour through two years of labor selling fish off a truck in suburbia before returning to higher education, philosophically firm . . . as a conservative. Professors, albeit enjoying the spar during class, exhibited no interest in my offer of an ideologically divergent protégé. And, in any case, the graduate schools to which I applied en route to the life of a college professor looked past the encouraging evidence of grades, standardized test scores, and recommendations, to the subversive fealty to tradition and common sense, conveyed in my writing samples. In them, they found excuse to deny my applications.

Forced back into the working world, I accepted my allotted gray office cubicle outside of Boston and rehearsed the polite redirection of conversation when others wrongly assumed that I was of like mind.

Self-expression I buried in a rotating stack of manuscripts, sending poetry and fiction to be rejected and returned and sent and rejected and returned. With frustration thus wound, I once again spun away from the assistance of others and took to self-publishing literary reviews for a local writers' group to which I belonged—editing, designing, fundraising, and printing each edition almost entirely on my own initiative.

Through that effort, I glimpsed the world that awaits those willing to scrape away the frictional aspects of their worldviews and slip smoothly into a cultural Lethe. Public grants, donations, and sympathetic advertising might float to those who take care not to ripple the waters, and I must confess a deep temptation to be still. When 9/11 thrust political convictions to the tip of my pen, however, the tide turned me away.

It would deny reality, of course, to insist that rigid conformity ceases at ideological boundaries. Human beings are naturally more comfortable among those with whom we agree, and with limited resources to sort all candidates, such comfort will always bear on the chosen beneficiaries of our opportunities. But those paths toward which I've always inclined, the clichéd "roads less traveled," our culture has long characterized as pursuits of the Left, and the redoubts of open-mindedness and overt independence—in the arts, in academia, in media—have been jealously guarded.

Nonconformity, if it is not to be synonymous with perpetual adolescence and social disengagement, depends on principles that are now to the right of center. Innovation requires an emphasis on merit-driven results, determined by the mechanisms of a free market. By contrast, direct authorities—central planners and experts—who allocate resources and determine individuals' roles in the society inevitably mandate conformity, even if their banner recalls a rebel pose. Look only to the unbroken theme of the modern antihero—self-destructive habits—for evidence that a constitutional conformity, not individual self-realization, is the objective of the secular progressive movement.

The truly self-reliant must adhere to a deeper reality, with threads whose value they understand more as a matter of faith than of comprehension. They must master the language in order to speak an elegant rebellion more profound than empty statements of "I rebel." They must determine how a structure resists the forces that would destroy it before they can challenge the principles of its construction. And they must feel the unique human heartbeat behind each exertion in order to believe in the competence of the individual in the first place.

Such heartbeats practically throbbed beneath my hands in the timbers of that old mansion by the sea. Crawling through the barely passable corridors of the elaborate roof system, cutting holes for the modern mechanisms of climate control, I was warmed, as it were, by the very breaths of men whose hands had been the last to touch the rafters generations before, not long after the United States' internal war of unity and freedom and not long before the next century turned toward atrocities of central planning and inhuman calculations of human worth.

By the nature of his work, the carpenter has an experiential understanding that he cannot disregard the traditions of his craft. He values them as the very air he breathes, else the structure will collapse. By virtue of his labor, he also knows that no nail is driven of its own volition, and in volition exists personality.

The windows that provided me cold light for my work were once the cherished task of the workshop. Each sash had its fine details and tightly fit joints, ensconced in careful balances of measurement and weight to be functional. The wood and glass, pointed and glazed against the weather, were balanced across pulleys with iron cylinders hidden within the hollow jambs. Behind each detail was a man saddle-sitting at his bench, tapping carefully shaped chisels. With each opening and closing, the rattle of the weights speaks of the window's maker and lifetimes of experience, though even his grandchildren have gone to their graves.

Interpreting the manner of construction, I concluded that the crew installed the windows as they stacked the walls of stone and brick, attaching strips of wood on both sides before fitting the frames into their openings. As the masons completed each level of the structure, they'd pour concrete along the windows' sides, securing them in place with mud that would turn to stone around wooden strips. It was the evidence of the workers that gave the method away: if the laborer had poured too little water into the concrete mix, air gaps remained toward the bottom of the window because the mixture clumped rather than flowed. If his mix had been too wet, the concrete bled out beneath. Even in such simple activities, we cannot help but leave our marks.

So, let some well-heeled transcendentalist proclaim that nonconformity is the precondition of self-fulfillment. He provides but the last link of the chain: it is, in turn, a precondition of nonconformity to *do* something; in doing something, one must necessarily conform to steps and strategies learned and taught, and judging well among the possibilities is itself an exercise in conformity with criteria of wisdom.

Across the centuries, the truth has remained that an infant is not, in fact, self-reliant but wholly reliant, and the adults will tire of cooing for the child's entertainment if he or she fails to mature. We, the newly grown, can hope that prior generations' experiment in inverted lessons of maturity will fade to echoes once we turn from the walls that they've exposed and seek an outward view. Then, in true and good nonconformity, we can rebuild.

8

THE CONSISTENCY OF GAY CONSERVATIVES

James Kirchick

In the prologue to his 1992 memoir *Coming Out Conservative*, the late political activist Marvin Liebman recounts an experience that all gay people face. One of the most important organizational brains behind the conservative movement (he was a founder of both Young Americans for Freedom and the American Conservative Union), Liebman was spending the 1976 Thanksgiving weekend at the Connecticut home of his close friends William and Pat Buckley. Joining them was Ronald Reagan, who earlier that year had conceded his primary campaign for president to Gerald Ford, along with his wife, Nancy, and son, Ron. With Buckley, Liebman, and Reagan, assembled in the kitchen that evening was the nation's conservative brain trust.

Over a nightcap and out of the hearing of the wives and children, Reagan expressed his concern that Ron, a student at Yale, had taken up ballet dancing. "I haven't told Nancy yet, but young Ron has told me he's going to quit Yale and become a . . . ballet dancer. Now I don't care what the kid does as long as it's legal and makes him happy, but . . ." Turning to Liebman, Reagan asked, "But aren't dancers . . . aren't dancers sort of . . . funny?"

Enduring an ignorant or bigoted statement about homosexuality—and Reagan's naive search for a polite way to insinuate homosexuality was certainly more the former than the latter—is something that every gay person experiences at some point in their life. How they respond is determined by several factors, not the least of which are the assertiveness of the individual and how comfortable they are acknnowledging their homosexuality. Liebman, who was deeply closeted at the time and would not come out publicly until nearly fifteen years after this incident, tried to answer in as straightforward and discreet a way as possible. "I told him that some ballet dancers were 'funny,' of course, but that many were not," Liebman recalled, before reassuring the future president that Mikhail Baryshnikov "was one of the sex idols of our time, immensely attractive to women."

Numerous studies have shown, and common sense suggests, that people who know a gay person personally are more accepting of homosexuality and supportive of the panoply of concerns called "gay rights" than those who do not. Reagan had many gay friends from his time in Hollywood (Rock Hudson, most famously, among them), and Nancy, like many women of her station and glamour, could call upon a vast array of confirmed bachelors as "walkers." As for Liebman's secret, Reagan "must certainly have known," but neither man was prepared to discuss it. "Denial can be a peaceful form of retreat," Liebman wrote, an observation that described its author as much as it did the insurgent conservative political star.

If hearing the veiled (and sometimes not-so-veiled) homophobic slight is universal to the gay experience, it is something that gay conservatives, especially those in the fields of media and politics, must deal with on a more profound basis. For being gay is not unlike being conservative, in that both, I believe, are an expression of an individual's most basic humanity. To be sure, one's political viewpoints can and almost always do evolve, in a way that one's sexuality does not (as someone who canvassed for Ralph Nader's 2000 presidential campaign, I can easily attest to this phenomenon). But for those of us right-of-center gay people who take politics seriously and see it as the expression of deeply felt values, arguing on behalf of causes in which we genuinely don't believe would be like trying to make love to someone of the opposite gender. In this sense, politics is very much about human nature.

Reading Liebman's memoir evoked a similar encounter I had with a prominent conservative writer while I was a senior in college. Like Liebman, I had begun making something of a name for myself in right-of-center circles with my columns in the *Yale Daily News*, and I found myself one evening at a gathering of prominent conservatives in New York City. Talking with a well-known conservative writer about Islamic Jihadism, I noted the hypocrisy of some European Leftists who claimed to believe in gay rights yet had no problem forming political alliances with Muslim reactionaries who backed harsh penalties, even violent ones, for homosexuality. What united these strange bedfellows, I observed, was a shared hatred of America and capitalism. Not a particularly original thought, but one to which conservatives, most of whom didn't much care for gay rights, were not attuned.

Expecting to earn confirmation for my detecting this most basic, and really quite heinous example of liberal insincerity, I was taken aback when my interlocutor told me that he was actually "sympathetic" to much of what Islamists had to say about homosexuality. Indeed, it wasn't their views on homosexuality that bothered him, but rather their militant opposition to America and its overseas interests that put them beyond the pale.

Now, unlike Marvin Liebman at the point of his conservative kitchen-cabinet anecdote, I was long (well, three years) out of the closet, had written numerous articles in which I discussed my own homosexuality (including articles for the gay press), and readily assumed that most people familiar with my work—as this individual certainly was—knew I was gay. But whether he actually did or not matters only in the judgment of just how hostile was his response.

Aghast at what I had heard, I took another gulp of my drink and said nothing. I knew that there was plenty of antigay sentiment in the conservative world—this was only two years after the unsuccessful attempt to insert an amendment into the United States Constitution, banning gay marriage—but I did not expect to confront it at so prestigious a gathering. So naked, not to mention extreme, an expression of homophobia was something one heard at assemblies of the Christian Coalition or fringe groups exclusively devoted to rolling back the political progress gays had made, not in the refined precincts of intellectual conservatism into which I was readily ascending. When the writer—who, up until that point, was a significant influence on my own work (I have rarely read him in the years since)—walked away, all I could do was complain to a straight female friend, the only other witness to the exchange. But my sense of confused anger was only compounded when, later that evening, the main speaker took a tangential swipe at gays "making a mockery of marriage."

Looking back on this episode, I can confidently say that were I to find myself in a similar situation today (and, much to my surprise, I have not, which in its own small way says much about the progress that the country, and the conservative movement especially, has made in an incredibly short period of time), I would not react in the cowardly way in which I did. As Liebman wrote of his sixty-seven years as a closeted homosexual, I regretted my "compliant silence" in the face of such an illiberal sentiment, which was in its own, momentary way a form of being in the "closet."

The private, offhand remarks of individuals are one thing. The public policy positions of a movement or political party are another. And while I've largely avoided personalized homophobia in my relatively short time associating with conservatives, that does not mean that the conservative movement is devoid of it. My positive experience is attributable to several factors, among them the fact that most people are averse to confrontation, and even those who consider homosexuality anathema are unlikely to say something rude to someone they know to be gay. It may also be due to the fact that many of my conservative friends and acquaintances are libertarian, taking the view that the government should adopt no position whatsoever when it comes to homosexuality. I also have not traveled extensively to the red-state American heartland, where the base of the Republican Party comes from and where views about homosexuality are more retrograde than those held by the intellectual conservatives of New York and Washington.

Whatever the negative views that some conservatives hold about gay people, I have certainly received more vitriol from Leftists for my right-of-center opinions. I believe the source of this anger is the same that drives so many people on the Left to vilify black and female conservatives. The Left views gays, like ethnic minorities and women, not as individuals but as part of an oppressed group. And because the Left (at least in word) supports gay rights, it is therefore the duty of each and every homosexual to sign up with the checklist of liberal policies. Indeed, a gay (or black or Latino) person who does not adopt a Left-wing worldview is showing the worst form of ingratitude, as we "owe" the Left for any of the rights that we enjoy.

It may sound paradoxical, but the "gay agenda" today is fundamentally conservative. Neither gay activists nor movement conservatives will be happy to admit this, but it is inescapable. Those in the conservative movement most resistant to making peace with the main criteria of this agenda—the extension of civil marriage rights to homosexuals, the right to serve openly in the military, the right to adopt children, and the acceptance of homosexuality itself as a benign, naturally occurring quality of the human race—continue to think of the gay rights movement as it was in its heyday of the immediate post-Stonewall era. They see gay people as threats to the traditional American family structure and social order, which, to be perfectly fair, most of the prominent gay activists of the mid-twentieth century were. They had no interest in monogamous marriage, which they viewed as patriarchic and misogynistic.

But today, there are no calls for free love and the right to keep bathhouses open. The young gay activists protesting in the streets of California do so in order to get married. They want to join this bedrock institution, not tear it apart. In this, they are assuming the mantle of those who took part in the 1969 Stonewall riots, which were sparked when a gay bar's patrons refused to continue enduring harassment at the hands of New York City Police Department. Though considered part of the counterculture, which in most respects it certainly was, the modern gay rights movement was galvanized by calls to one of the most basic constitutional principles: freedom of association.

The same goes for service in the military. In the 1960s and 1970s, gay activists were rooting for Vietcong victory and voyaging to Cuba to help realize Fidel Castro's Communist revolution. Today, a major demand of the country's most prominent gay groups is the right to *join* the United States military so as to strengthen the caliber of the armed forces. Such positions would be unimaginable to many of the gay activists of the early years, who, with some notable exceptions, were down-the-line hard-Leftists.

As for the condition of same-sex attraction itself, the belief that it is unchangeable and determined either in the womb or not long after birth returns our understanding of homosexuality to the place where it belongs: science. This naturalistic explanation of homosexuality is at odds with the claims of Left-wing "queer" theorists, who argue that binary sexuality is a social construct, something forced upon us by a conservative society adhering to strict definitions of gender roles, and that homosexuality is "performative." On this, the reactionaries and radicals oddly agree. But homosexuality is no more a choice than is the color of one's skin or eyes. A rational society finds a way to deal with it in a humane and productive way, not pretend it doesn't exist.

It is for these reasons that I see no conflict whatsoever in the tenets of conservatism and a "progressive" understanding of homosexuality, nor in being a gay conservative. It is, rather, certain critical constituencies within the conservative movement that have made the designation so difficult for many to comprehend, and perhaps harder for its designees to bear. But there is nothing inherently oxymoronic in a gay conservative. There is no reason why one's sexual and romantic attraction to members of the same sex should render one predisposed to a Left-wing view about the power of public employees' unions, or late-term abortion, or affirmative action. Indeed, one could even argue, and some gay conservatives have, that on the latter two questions, being gay informs a right-of-center disposition. What will the gay rights establishment have to say about abortion if medical advancements bring about the ability to discern a gay gene in fetuses? And while the prospect of employment and admissions preferences for sexual minorities may today seem like a wild idea (though not really so wild, given the Left-wing tilt of contemporary academia), does a realistic survey of affirmative action and the resentment it has caused on the campus and in the workplace instill optimism for those who wish to see gay people fully integrated in society?

After the crushing blow of AIDS and the maturation of the first sexually liberated generation of gays, it was only a matter of time that a new, more nuanced, gay politics would emerge. In the 1990s, a small group of right-of-center writers and thinkers—most prominently, Bruce Bawer, Jonathan Rauch, and Andrew Sullivan—began positing some ideas that many in the gay commentariat and intelligentsia considered heretical. The purpose of their intellectual campaign was to both integrate gay people into mainstream American society and make room in mainstream American society for gay people's integration, to give gay people "a place at the table" (the title of Bawer's path-breaking book on the subject).

But these writers, while vilified by the activist gay Left and most of the Right (which patronized them for their earnest but ultimately fruitless efforts to seek acceptance), did not so much *create* a gay conservatism as express the viewpoints of a silent majority. It's true that the most visible aspects of gay culture up until the 1980s had been those of hedonism, frivolity, and promiscuity. And in the minds of most straight people, this is what it meant to be gay. But there was, and always has been, a great mass of gay people who live lives no different from their straight peers. And there is no reason for them to be more Left-wing in their political orientation other than that they are members of a long-persecuted class. As gay life becomes more bourgeois and the legal restrictions gay people face are gradually lifted, the justifications for gay radicalism will disappear just as the reasons for gay conservatism will multiply.

Rather, it is the geographic structure of the contemporary American conservative movement, so dependent upon the votes of religious conservatives (particularly evangelical Christians in the South), which makes so many gay people and their straight allies view the Republican Party with hostility. It was the religious Right, imbued with an undeniable hostility to gay people, which gave the conservative movement political power. Today, the GOP base remains opposed to gay marriage, but while the occasional Republican politician may utter an ignorant remark here or there about homosexuality, antigay animus is slowly dissipating. It does not, for example, appear to have any place in the Tea Party movement sweeping the country. At the 2008 Republican National Convention, 49 percent of the delegates supported civil unions or marriage for gays, a number that will likely increase every four years as the delegate pool becomes younger, itself a reflection of the remarkable generational shift that has occurred in the past decade on the issues surrounding homosexuality.

Though he would renounce the term (if not the philosophical holds) of conservatism just five years later, Marvin Liebman was onto something in his 1990 "coming out" letter to William F. Buckley Jr., published in the pages of *National Review*. "The conservative view," he declared, "based as it is on the inherent rights of the individual over the state, is the logical political home of gay men and women." The majority of gay people would find this claim baffling. But rest assured the day is coming when they will not.

9

SEEING THE LIGHT IN SEVENTH GRADE

Evan Coyne Maloney

My political epiphany came in a tile classroom on the top floor of a building that the New York City public school system referred to as Junior High School 167.

At the time, I was old enough to know I was fascinated by politics, but too young to have figured out my own opinions. My views, insofar as they could truly be considered mine, were default views, absorbed from my family, television, and the surroundings in liberal Manhattan.

One day, my teacher announced that each student would have to prepare a three-minute talk on a current events topic and present it in front of the whole class. My assigned topic was nuclear disarmament.

Although the Soviet Union would soon crumble, the Cold War was America's main existential threat at the time. Ronald Reagan was president, and nuclear scare stories were still a staple of network television.

When it came to the topic I was assigned, I had picked up enough signals from my environment to understand that nuclear weapons were Bad, and, therefore, to be Good was to favor the elimination of those weapons.

I believed I was a Good Person, so naturally I shared the same political views as other Good People. No further thinking was required. This presentation was going to be a piece of cake!

Eventually, deadline day came and the teacher started calling students at random. As I sat with my hands tensely clasped inside my desk, butterflies began fluttering inside my stomach. Each time another name was called, my heart accelerated to the point of near-explosion until enough sound escaped the teacher's lips for me to recognize that it was not my turn. Whew! Dodged a bullet.

But then I remembered I still wasn't off the hook, and now I had to endure three more minutes of another goofball kid droning on about the space shuttle, acid rain, or endangered tree frogs.

Finally, my name was called.

My heart skipped a beat and the world stopped. As I pushed my seat back from my desk, life slowly spun back into full speed. I stood up, walked to the front of the room, and went on autopilot.

I talked passionately about our Republican president, that dangerous cowboy, and how worried I was that his ancient finger hovered over the nuclear launch button. I spoke about peace and how we could achieve it if only we had the courage to get rid of our weapons. I promoted peaceful coexistence and mutual understanding; if only we were more tolerant and kind, maybe the Soviets would stop seeing us as enemies. I whined a plea to the adults of America, imploring them to Please Think of the Children, because We Are the Future!

About halfway through, it occurred to me that I didn't believe a damn thing I was saying.

The Soviet Union had nuclear weapons pointed at us. So if we got rid of ours, how would that make us safer? Would the Soviets really give up their weapons just because we did? I may only have been approaching pubescence, but I certainly wasn't that naive.

This realization was happening at an inconvenient time. I was halfway through giving a speech I now thought was bullshit. I started fumbling my words. The index cards in my hands started to shake.

But I had a presentation to finish, and the only words available to me were the ones on those cards. All I wanted was to be done with it so I could sit down and cope with my cognitive dissonance. So I sheepishly followed my scrawled talking points, the ones I now regarded as lies.

Only later did I recognize the significance of that little speech: that's when I stood up a liberal, and sat down a conservative.

This episode also opened my eyes to something else: the social dynamic that leads to groupthink, the propensity for people to adopt opinions from those around them rather than through their own critical thinking.

If a person hasn't thought very much about a given topic, if it's something they're not terribly passionate about, that person will tend to reflect the views that they hear expressed most frequently by people they like, respect, or want to emulate. The more often people are exposed to a particular line of thinking through their approved channels, the more likely they are to adopt those views without much thought.

That's what led to my classroom epiphany. By the time I was in junior high, I hadn't spent any considerable time thinking about the political implications of nuclear weapons, but the people I looked up to all seemed to have the same views on the subject. Because I hadn't really ever been exposed to contrary positions from trusted sources, I had no reason to spend any time thinking about it. Their opinions became my opinions, by default.

Given the sheer volume of information our world generates every day, the dynamic behind groupthink makes perfect sense. If we tried to carefully think through every concept we're ever exposed to, we'd be in a constant state of analysis paralysis. It simply isn't feasible to approach absolutely everything in life as a hypothesis needing to be scientifically proven. So, we quite naturally adopt thoughts from those around us, thereby short-circuiting the need for our own analysis.

When dealing with provable matters of fact, this saves us a lot of time and annoyance. Without even realizing it, we accept the concepts of gravity and acceleration and are generally content to assume that jumping off the top of a skyscraper is more dangerous than jumping off the couch.

Opinions are a different matter entirely. Once a critical mass of a community begins sharing the same opinions, those opinions get socially transmitted in the same way that facts do. But opinions are not facts, and groupthink doesn't account for this distinction. Groupthink merely demands thought conformity, and when it runs amok, dissenters start getting punished. To see this in action, look no further than the typical college campus.

Today, the core of academia suffers from the rot of political correctness, the belief that certain political opinions are inherently correct or incorrect. Nowadays, many professors believe their role is to ensure that students graduate with the "correct" set of views.

Enforcing the correctness of opinions is something dictators do, and the toxic combination of groupthink and political correctness has turned many American campuses into prisons of the mind, places where even the mildest speech can get you in a whole mess of trouble.

I directed a documentary film called *Indoctrinate U* that looks at groupthink and how it can lead school officials to punish people who hold disfavored opinions. In making the film, I spoke with students, professors, and administrators all over the country at every level of academia. I visited dozens of schools, from Ivies to small private campuses, from big state schools to tiny community colleges. No matter where I went, at each of these schools, the environment was virtually identical: Left-wing political views were favored, and anything else could be grounds for punishment.

Republicans and conservatives aren't the only ones who run afoul of the thought police. Libertarians, independents, religious Christians and Jews, and even liberal Democrats have gotten into trouble for straying from the flock.

One of the more appalling cases in *Indoctrinate U* occurred at California Polytechnic State University in San Luis Obispo. Cal Poly, as it's commonly known, is a part of the California State University system. As such, it is legally a part of the state government, which means that if Cal Poly interferes with constitutionally protected speech in any way, the school is breaking the law.

Against this backdrop of legal certitude, a former student named Steve Hinkle was subjected to harassment by the Cal Poly school administration for a year and a half, during which time he lived with the threat of expulsion hanging over his head while he was trying to successfully complete his coursework.

Steve unintentionally committed a thought crime: he posted a flyer announcing an upcoming speaking engagement.

The flyer itself was quite simple. Saying, "Come Hear Mason Weaver," it promoted an appearance by an author that the College

Republicans had invited to campus. Alongside a small picture of Mason Weaver, the flyer listed the date, time, and location of the event. The flyer's headline highlighted the title of Weaver's most recent book. Nothing else appeared on the flyer.

Although that seems rather benign, the apparent problem with the flyer was that the author happened to be black, and that his picture was shown alongside the title of his book, which happened to be *It's OK to Leave the Plantation*.

This imagery—despite being factually accurate—did not sit well with several students in Cal Poly's Multicultural Center. Never mind that Steve had a clear constitutional right to post the flyer. Never mind that the words were chosen by the man who was supposedly being degraded by them. What the flyer actually meant was beside the point; at Cal Poly, the primary concern was that the flyer offended someone.

Poor Steve Hinkle. If he had understood the power dynamics at play, he would have known that as a blond-haired, blue-eyed white male member of the College Republicans, he was prejudged a racist long before he ever set foot in the Multicultural Center.

All this might be a bit hard to understand if you haven't spent much time on college campuses in the last few decades. So perhaps I should explain a few concepts first.

As it is practiced in academia, multiculturalism holds that all cultures are equal, except Western culture, which has a history of oppression and war, and is therefore worse. All religions are equal, except Christianity and Judaism, which are both worse, because they informed the beliefs of the capitalist bloodsuckers who founded this racist, sexist, homophobic country. According to multiculturalism, all races are equal, except Caucasians, who long ago went into business with slave traders in Africa, and therefore they are worse. The genders, too, are equal, except for those paternalistic males, who with their testosterone, greed, and aggression have turned this planet into a polluted, war-torn living hell, so therefore they are worse.

Multiculturalism is a way of claiming to support equality while at the same time engaging in blatant discrimination. It is a philosophy that requires people to be sorted into groups so that a political pecking order may be established among them.

I call this the Hierarchy of Multiculturalism, and it is governed by these simple rules:

1. If a person is a member of a group guilty of past oppression (Oppressors), that person has no moral standing in relation to people in any group that's ever been victimized by those Oppressors (Victims).
2. Oppressors are always assumed to be guilty in relation to Victims.
3. An Oppressor can only avoid presumed guilt by expressing agreement with the political aims of those who claim to speak for the Victims.
4. Working on behalf of those political aims is the only way for Oppressors to redeem their inherent immorality.
5. Victims can lose their moral standing by expressing a preference for individual rights instead of group rights.
6. A Victim who comes to the defense of an Oppressor is a traitor and is therefore even more morally repugnant than Oppressors themselves.

According to the Multicultural Hierarchy, the desires of Victims always take precedence over the rights of Oppressors. So it's no surprise that when a few students in the Multicultural Center objected to Steve's flyer, his constitutional rights no longer mattered; what mattered was that Victims were offended.

Steve's violation was twofold: not only was he an Oppressor, but he was promoting Mason Weaver, a black conservative who argued that self-reliance and free markets constituted "a new Underground Railroad" capable of lifting people out of poverty and weaning them from government dependence.

Mason Weaver represents the ultimate threat to the Multicultural Hierarchy because he points out the illusion of perpetual victimhood. Weaver was to be detested, because not only was he a shill for capitalism, but, as a black man, he was supposed to favor group rights at the expense of individual rights. But because he didn't, he's a sellout, an Uncle Tom, and a traitor to his race. And as such, he is to be even more reviled than Hinkle, who at least had no choice in the matter of being born a white male.

So, when Steve posted that Mason Weaver flyer, the students in the Multicultural Center did what any open-minded, tolerant people would do: they called the police.

Steve was gone by the time the police arrived, but the students filed a complaint anyway. One officer stated that the Multicultural Center reported "a suspicious white male passing out literature of an offensive racial nature."

Eventually, Steve became identified as the "suspicious white male" in question. But even after the students in the Multicultural Center were explained the meaning of the flyer, they pressed on with their complaint.

Faced with angry Victims, the administrators at Cal Poly did what administrators at many schools do: they bent over backward to appease the Victims, even if it meant branding one of their own students a racist and trampling on his First Amendment rights. The Victims demanded that Cal Poly punish the Oppressor, and the school began disciplinary proceedings against Hinkle.

Even in the midst of final exams, the school pulled Steve into various meetings and disciplinary hearings, one of which lasted more than seven hours. For a while, even though Steve had been threatened with expulsion, the charges against him weren't quite clear. At times, the school subjected him to questioning by an attorney, but Steve was allowed no legal representation of his own. The school's strategy seemed to be to get Steve to talk as much as possible and hope he would say something incriminating that could be used to justify a punishment.

But it wasn't working, and eventually the school realized it had a problem: in order to punish Steve, they needed to charge him with something. They knew he couldn't be disciplined for the content of the flyer; it was constitutionally protected speech. After a while, the administrators decided to charge Steve with "disrupting a campus event."

The original student complaints couldn't support a charge of disrupting a campus event. There was no record of any campus event in the Multicultural Center during the time Steve was there. None of the students mentioned an event at all, much less one being disrupted, and they never characterized Steve's behavior in a way that could be considered remotely disruptive.

A newer angle was needed, one that would bolster the disruption claim. The new logic was even more tenuous. The police arrived at the Multicultural Center some time later, after Steve was gone. Because there was a scheduled meeting in the Multicultural Center when the police entered, the students claimed that their arrival constituted a disruption. But it was Steve who was held responsible for the supposed disruption, not the students who actually called the police.

Eventually, Steve contacted the Foundation for Individual Rights in Education (FIRE), which helped get media attention for the case. National coverage came from CNN, Fox News, and the *Los Angeles Times*. The absurdity of the case was obvious for all to see, and Cal Poly became a national laughingstock.

FIRE also helped Steve find a lawyer. Steve's legal representation was provided by the Center for Individual Rights, a nonprofit law firm that filed suit against Cal Poly in federal court.

Thanks to the negative media attention and the added pressure of a lawsuit, after putting Steve Hinkle through eighteen months of disciplinary hearings and legal maneuvers, Cal Poly listened to the advice of a federal judge, finally recognized that they had a losing case, and threw in the towel. They dropped all charges against Steve, cleared his disciplinary record, and agreed to pay a $40,000 settlement.

Steve prevailed in the end, but he paid a huge personal price. A large chunk of his college career was scarred by the daily agony of wondering whether he was about to be expelled. Meanwhile, Steve walked around campus branded a racist by the Multicultural Center and the administrators at his own school.

Steve's student accusers paid no price at all. Neither did the Cal Poly administrators, who spent hundreds of man-hours and obscene amounts of taxpayer money in their quest to destroy Steve Hinkle.

The only price paid by Cal Poly was the damage to the school's reputation. The original public backlash was devastating, and each time *Indoctrinate U* appears on TV, a new round of negative attention is cast on the school.

The Steve Hinkle case was one of the reasons I wanted to make *Indoctrinate U*. It was a perfect illustration of what can go wrong when groupthink takes over an institution: fairness, logic, and basic decency all go out the window in an attempt to enforce thought-conformity.

The only way to cure academia of groupthink is to combat it with intellectual diversity. Diversity of thought is not just something that should be a rallying cry of libertarians and conservatives; it should be supported by everyone who values a rigorous education. And, if only for selfish reasons, today's academic tyrants should be careful with their power: their views may not always dominate. Creating an environment that doesn't tolerate dissent could end up backfiring some day.

In the mid-1800s, a potato famine in Ireland led to an estimated 1 million deaths of starvation. The famine was caused when *Phytophthora infestans*, a potato blight, spread across Ireland and led to widespread crop failures. But the seed of the problem was a lack of diversity.

Before the famine hit, each successive potato crop in Ireland had been grown using agricultural clones of the previous generation of potatoes. Certain varieties became favored, and, over time, potatoes were grown from an ever-smaller universe of plant strains. Eventually, the gene pool stagnated, and most of the potatoes in Ireland shared common genetic code.

Because most of the potatoes were essentially the same, they possessed the same vulnerabilities. There may have been many strains resilient to the form of potato blight that swept Ireland during the famine years, but they had been weeded out by man's unnatural selection. So, when *Phytophthora infestans* hit Ireland, crops of the country's main food staple were destroyed for years on end. And, as a tragic result, a million people starved to death.

Today, the lack of intellectual diversity in academia has left it vulnerable to the most destructive tendencies of its own ideology. One astounding aspect of the Hinkle case is that at no time did anyone in a position of power at Cal Poly put a stop to the injustice being done.

The disease of groupthink led administrators to do serious damage to the school's reputation. If Cal Poly had treated intellectual diversity as seriously as they treated diversity of appearance, rational minds would have recognized the flyer for the innocent event announcement that it was, and there never would have been such a thing as "the Hinkle case" perpetually tarnishing Cal Poly's name.

The Achilles heel of groupthink it that people under its spell always end up doing something stupid and thuggish. And, as a result, they're constantly exposing their own behavior for what it is.

When that happens, it must be fought. But when it's all over, sometimes the best response is just to point and laugh. Groupthink requires a perception of power, and that perception can't survive sustained derision.

At public screenings of *Indoctrinate U*, one of the scenes that gets the most laughter is my attempt to question the president of Cal Poly in his office. Instead, I was blocked by one of the president's flunkies, a short, mumbling, mealy-mouthed man whose manner of speech was so mellow and monotone that he makes Senator Harry Reid sound like Robin Williams.

In the film, this gentleman became the living embodiment of Cal Poly. And boy, does he make people laugh!

It may take many years to bring intellectual diversity back to higher ed. But in the meantime, small victories can be won by shining a light on the offenders. Video recording equipment is cheap enough now to be within the reach of many people; most reasonably modern home computers are powerful enough to edit video, and, often, simple video-editing software comes preinstalled.

I hope my film is the beginning of a trend on a thousand campuses. Students, grab your cameras and point them at your tormentors! Make them defend what they know they cannot. Hit them with some of that *South Park* snark, and upload it all to YouTube.

If there's one thing a power-tripping academic's ego can't stand, it's full-throated mockery.

10

MAN UP

Katherine Miller

"We live in more of a pussy generation now," Clint Eastwood told *Esquire* magazine last year. "[E]verybody's become used to saying, 'Well, how do we handle it psychologically?' "

Eastwood tells truths. America's elite has a problem. It's skinny jeans and scarves, it's Bama bangs and pants with tiny, tiny embroidered lobsters, it's Michael Cera, it's guys who compliment a girl's dress by brand, it's guys who don't know who bats fourth for the Yankees. Between the hipsters and the fratstars, American intellectual men under the age of twenty-five have lost track of acting like Men—and these are our future leaders. We have no John Wayne, no Clint Eastwood. And girls? Girls hate it.

This all occurred to me at 1:47 a.m. on November 8, 2008. I was on the phone in a hotel hallway, listening to this guy moan about this girl that didn't want to get it get it, if you will. Out of some cruel, dazzling dark corner of my metal heart, a single thought formulated: Man up.

Intellectual elite girls know this secret. Vanderbilt University stands near the light end of a two-decade tunnel from Southern Playground of the Rich to generic Duke stepsister, but the tunnel produced a foil to the unmanned masses: the 2000s Vandy Girl. Embodied most in a handful of elite sororities, the concept of Vandy Girl requires one shot of the Old Spirit (pearls and champagne and knowing what to say and when to say it), and two shots of this confidence that's a tic-tac-toe board of goals and timelines.

So, the calculus goes, the girls isolate aspects of masculinity—the drive, the confidence—in lightning rounds of Natural Selection Yahtzee. The men, likewise, drift to the center. They soften. They become Euro basketball players who never played high school ball, falling down like they've been shot after every hand check, and telling you they don't feel respected. Don't feel respected? Feel? I wouldn't trust that person in a crisis. Why can't we all shift in one direction, instead of stumbling into an androgynous mass of feelings-first zombie groupthink?

But perhaps you don't believe me. Maybe you live in some neo-noir situation where the men smoke on dark corners or in open plains and don't wear scarves unless it's cold enough to cut a hole in some ice and pull a fish out, and even then are a little hesitant about the whole thing. I don't know your life.

They're not bad guys, not necessarily, this First Team All-Sister Mary Margaret. They're generally polite, they love their parents, they get good grades at excellent schools. But underneath this sheen of the Good Kid, the Good Kind, thought overcomes action, and emotion overcomes thought.

"It's selfishness," my high school principal explained to me. He grew up in Western Pennsylvania and commands respect, whether at my privileged high school, or at his new, post-retirement post at a far rougher school. "It comes down to two questions: 'What have you done for me lately?' and 'How will this look?' "

Vanity over pride, selfishness over self-restraint—serious problems that can be traced from one to the next, streaks of light in the dark forming one big circuit.

The Sports Enthusiast can recite Yankee batting averages like the alphabet, but can't explain the infield fly rule. He doesn't know what he doesn't know, but he was recently hired by a top-tier consulting firm. Fratastic can thrill a girl with Lost Generation levels of raging and fluent French, but in between tequila shots, he'll judge anyone with a harshness that stings. The Moderate refuses to subscribe to a political ideology, so he meticulously eschews conservative bigotry and liberal recklessness by calling himself a Joe Lieberman Guy. He knows his politics, but he doesn't want to take a stand.

Then we have the cavalry, aggregated into a single figure: Backstreet Boy X, who earns his title with all the violent action of a sleeping kitten. Joseph Gordon-Levitt's character, Tom, in *(500) Days of Summer* captures Backstreet Boy X perfectly: smitten, ironic, and emotional. Backstreet Boy No. 3 lit candles, placed rose petals just so, and waited in a dark room on Valentine's Day for a girl who'd already said no—and then refused to talk to her the rest of the year. Backstreet Boy No. 16 informed his girlfriend of three months when he would propose. Backstreet Boy No. 28 refused to talk to his girlfriend for an entire day after she forgot to reply to his "have a good day" text.

A 2008 *New York Observer* piece categorized a special serial version of the Backstreet Boys as the Homme Fatale.

"He was sensitive, funny, supersmart, not athletic at all and not physically imposing," one actress explained. "But there was something that was so charismatic—a gentleness and gracefulness and a confidence."

Backstreet's back, all right? Boom. The article goes on to document the trail of unconsummated, unsatisfying, undefined faux-relationships all these sensitive, creative men left behind. Maybe we reap the product of socialist grade-school Valentines in Backstreet Boy X: everyone was supposed to feel special, and so everyone does. Rather than confront the more complex cultural issue, though, the article casts the Homme Fatale as a state of emotional mental illness; one man interviewed even calls the Homme Fatale an emotional sociopath. Addiction, anxiety, and depression always trump a well-placed, old-school "Man Up."

Feelings matter first, now. My principal coached the Little League team his son, Scott, played on when he was twelve. Scott was catching and a kid got hit by a pitch, fell to the ground, and rolled around crying. Scott looks at him and says something like "You're embarrassing yourself. Get up, pussy." The umpire immediately calls time, and tells my principal he needs to talk to him.

"I asked, 'Which one? The one embarrassing himself or the catcher?' " He admitted he and a few other parents of boys on the baseball team were probably too tough on their boys. "The kid who got hit with the pitch is a produce manager at a grocery store. Not that a produce manager is a bad job, but the three boys we were so tough on—one's a CPA, one's an attorney, and one's a captain in the Marines."

A couple months after the Great Hotel Epiphany of Man Up, I was killing time in the newspaper office, and the opinion editor needed a pinch-hitter for a column. So, what the hell, why not "Man Up, Vanderbilt"? A few hundred words later—on the prayer of the American college girl that the real world whittles down the anthropomorphized box of Easter peeps with whom we've gone to college—and I had forty e-mails, half a dozen comments, one response column, and a slew of passing thoughts from people I only sort of knew. Man Up is a cherry bomb met with evangelical fervor.

The column itself was a thrown-together list of superficial attributes. Don't have bangs, don't wear driving shoes (for fifteen dollars more, you can get the whole shoe!), and so on. And, of course, I did a few stupid things too in that column, choosing sort of arbitrary positives: I announced that fighting is hot, and I stipulated that real guys hunt and fish. Both obscure the spirit of the problem at hand; shooting a six-point buck requires no more masculinity than choosing Busch beer at 7-Eleven.

Nevertheless, the sentiment resonated. A Vandy grad and army captain stationed in Iraq ("218th Sand Dune on the Left") told me how glad he was to leave the pastels behind. One girl I'd taken a class with told me they'd put the column on the Theta house refrigerator during rush week. Another girl, a grad, killed the dreams of many: "Even post-college I can assure you they still love their pretty pastel shirts and diet sodas." Frat author Tucker Max bookmarked the link with the charm-heavy comment, "I am going to Vandy and fucking three hundred girls in a week."

Casually, quite a few people will commit to the Eastwood paradigm. You can play a round of Real Men Do Not faster than a round of dirty Scrabble. With the e-mail and Twitter entries I received while writing this, we can play one right now.

Real men do not: drink daiquiris; encroach on personal space or the splash zone; cry during *While You Were Sleeping*; cry at all, unless a wife, family member, or favorite dog has passed away; wear tight pants; do yoga; do theater or especially theatre; shop for themselves (moms, girlfriends, wives, and daughters do that); write poetry; wear eyeliner unless they're in an 80s rock band (a good one); highlight their hair; drive smart cars; use smiley faces in texts unless they're trying to get some ass; use the elliptical; or bring yogurt and a diet soda to work in a packed lunch.

Meanwhile, dark, tall, square-jawed actor Jon Hamm became a cultural icon as *Mad Men*'s Don Draper. More than two hundred thousand people added the Tebow Crying page on Facebook in a month. Dockers ran a fall 2009 campaign predicated on the perceived lack of masculinity: "Once upon a time, men wore the pants, and wore them well. Women rarely had to open doors and little old ladies never crossed the street alone. Men took charge because that's what they did. But somewhere along the way, the world decided it no longer needed men." Dodge worked up the same angle in their Super Bowl XLIV ad for the Charger, calling it Man's Last Stand. Suddenly, at the end of the first decade of this evolved twenty-first century, maybe a girl needs a little more than a fedora and an Animal Collective song to keep her warm at night.

Or maybe she doesn't. Not everyone loved this Man Up idea. You tell guys to stop wearing the man scarves in temperate Nashville, some woman will chime in with requests about how all women everywhere must now descend from the Twelve Oaks staircase, kitten out a three-syllable "Hi," and throw themselves on their husbands' funeral pyres in dresses stolen from Betty Draper.

One comment questioned my sacred femininity:

"I wonder how charitable you would be if a man suggested that your femininity was predicated on your ability to gracefully defer whatever education and dreams you have for your 'truly female' role as a homebound domestic manager and child-bearer who knows how to whip up a mean rack of lamb when the hubby brings the boss home for dinner?"

Marvel at fragile social framework in peril. If Bobby cuts his bangs, Jane must hood-slide into a Ford Pinto to escape college's reach and dream only of racks of lamb and hollandaise sauce. Shackled in some political correctness armistice, we back handspring straight into Meg March's kitchen if we consider damming the river.

"You may have to choose between a well-educated guy with a good job and warm personality," another comment chastised, "and a guy who can gut a fish and talk about sports after working on an oil rig. Just don't be surprised when this 'manly man' you craved expects you to conform to your own gender stereotypes (better be home with dinner ready in pearls and makeup with hair set up. And don't forget to smile and keep your mouth shut)."

Again, I think men can act like men and still be smart. I cannot believe this is such a novel concept to so many. It feels simple but this game of gender politics can stun you with its complexity. Our concept of masculinity functions as an inextricable product of our femininity; we live in this binary environment where only one well exists, and we can draw only so much water from it. If Bobby taps into his masculinity, Jane essentially sells herself to him. Rather than get all up in a hot-air balloon of pearl-clutching feelings, engaged in some Cold War of gender neutrality, can't we consider this question again: Why can't we all shift in one direction?

Vandy Girls know the secret, so we don't have to explain for them, but Man Up's kissing cousin—Sack Up, Ho—dictates a similar but distinctly ladylike set of ideals: Don't cry in public. Don't dance on a table (and, for Christ's sake, don't fall off of it). Don't be a tease. Don't ever proclaim that you "hate drama," because we all know exactly who starts the drama: it is you. Don't ever devolve to the point that sorority benefit or a bridal shower becomes both Waterloo and Thunderdome in your life. Contain your dignity and your shambles, and keep them to yourself. Sack up, ho.

TJ Miller would never say that, but he's comfortable with the idea. My father comes in at about five foot six, and has a habit of reading during Redskins games. He's a Silver Star, flew for the CIA, sold F-16s, and once got out of a mugging in the grocery store parking lot by hitting one of the muggers with a wine bottle. He's watched, basically, every Atlanta Braves game played in the last two decades, curses with vigor and finesse, and rotates through about five flannel shirts in the winter. He stands in our driveway smoking and went to Harvard Business School. He tells badass stories about FBI agents and professional baseball players, and all of my brother's friends are at least a little scared of him.

TJ Miller thinks we could all be tougher—he's just egalitarian that way. But he doesn't get to squint at Backstreet Boy X and spit "what the hell are you doing" or "don't tell people that" very frequently, so we have President Obama to mentor the androgynous flock instead. Comforting!

Now that I've dragged you to hell, out on some access road in a broken-down Range Rover with a boy sobbing because AAA won't pick up and his nerves are bad tonight, it's time for a game of chess. Or Monopoly Junior, whichever. Line up the First Team All-Sister Mary Margaret, choose your favorite, and let's predict the future.

A relationship can't just be a relationship. It has to be special. You need to feel good about it. "I don't mean to seem like I care about material things, like a social status," Animal Collective tells us, because, you know, God forbid.

A job can't just be a job. It has to be special. You need to feel good about it. The concept of the Global Citizen carries that allure for the

Sister Mary Margarets: citizenship begets duty, which begets opportunity, which begets action, which begets some overarching, uncontrollable force of Purpose. This is how Teach for America, mission work, and grad school win out over the unknown reality of banking, sales, or the military. Teach for America received 35,000 applications last year for 4,100 spots, because actually pursuing teaching certification would require a life decision. Even the top banking and consulting firms now brag about their rotations through the nonprofit sector, so Sister Mary Margaret can atone for selling out to the corporate overlords who tie all the free trade organic coffee bean farmers to railroad tracks.

But what if Man Up strikes back? The dominoes might be aligned. These Economic Times could kill the special, the Greatest Depression could pour Spic and Span all over these spilled feelings. More than half of workers aged eighteen to twenty-seven have been laid off since the financial crisis struck. Research by Microsoft, Fidelity, and Retail Financial Intelligence conducted over the past year indicates those in their late teens and early twenties may be the most financially conservative generation since those who lived through the Depression. A recent Harvard poll illustrated how Obama's devoted zombies might be turning into broken toy soldiers: "More young Americans now believe that the government's efforts will hurt (30 percent) rather than help (26 percent) their financial situation. The majority, 41 percent, say these efforts will have no impact." Slaying the feelings monster one open-handed sober Puritan slap of reality at a time! You need a Carter to get a Reagan!

I have hope in that embittered cynicism. For every Backstreet Boy X, for each Ironically Fratastic, I know a David, Dan, Matt, or Mike who's smart and still acts like a man. They do stupid things like stay up all night playing video games or wear duct-taped flip-flops instead of buying new ones. They also do things like call their grandfathers to check in or earn their tuition as work-study managers; they don't talk about the girls they've dated; they know their baseball; and they crack jokes about themselves. They have self-restraint and self-respect, and to them, I say, you'da you'da best.

To the rest, I say, man up. And yes, I realize this is all wildly bitchy, and one has to avoid sounding sour or angry about such things, because that is what an ugly woman would sound like. But then there's still a guy quoting *Gossip Girl* in his Facebook statuses, one telling a girl he can't date her because she might hate him if they break up, and one blowing bubbles at a picnic. Sometimes the truth has to be delivered. I'm just the mailman, delivering the mail.

11

LIBERALS ARE DUMB

And Other Shared Texts

Rachel Motte

Everyone knows that liberals are dumb. From social security to Sorkin, their endless harebrained schemes and subversive plots to corrupt your innocent children are eating away at the very foundation of our great nation—a nation that will eventually collapse because of their corruption, greed, and monstrous stupidity. The world would be a more wholesome place if liberals would simply give up their wicked ways and become good conservatives.

Right? Well, no, although, to hear many of the most popular conservative spokesmen, you might think so. It's a sad thing when an intellectual movement inspired by such high-caliber scholars as Edmund Burke and Milton Friedman is publicly reduced to the name-calling, overgeneralizations, and erroneous accusations represented above. If conservatism's future leaders would return to the old shared texts that so defined their forebears, we'd see not only a more effective group of activists but also a more viable movement—a movement with the potential to win not only short-term policy battles but also the hearts and minds of the American people. As it is now, I do wish more of my liberal friends would become conservatives, but I don't think the world will magically become a better place if they do. In fact, though I disagree with them, I have liberal friends who are decidedly more rational than some of my conservative friends. If liberals are stupid and wicked, they are no more so than a lot of the conservatives I've met.

When I was a teenager working in Washington, DC, I was surprised by how little many of my coworkers' lives differed from those of their liberal counterparts once the workday ended. You'd think that a day spent pondering and fighting for such treasures as the lives of unborn children, traditional marriages, and freedom of speech might change a man's habits once he's at home—and often it does. But not often enough.

For example, it's been frequently said that there are two kinds of people in Washington: those who get drunk and those who don't. It still strikes me as odd that this is true even within a movement so foundationally centered on the virtues of moderation and personal responsibility. There is nothing wrong with drinking, in and of itself, but drinking more than one can handle is at best irresponsible, and is arguably opposed to conservative ideals. That doesn't keep many conservatives from doing it. The same is true of other vices. Marital unfaithfulness is certainly opposed to the pro-family values many conservatives claim to espouse, but divorce rates are high across the board, and conservative public figures have definitely had their share of sex scandals. If anyone should know better, conservatives should—but if numbers are any indication, they don't.

Of course, there are major exceptions. Many fine people do great work in Washington, and I was privileged to spend time with a number of them. Morton Blackwell and then-Congressman Jim Ryun particularly stood out to me as good examples of the sort of humility and integrity one hopes to find among those who help determine our nation's future. I spent several months working for Congressman Ryun on Capitol Hill, and I quickly discovered that you can learn a lot about a man by watching the way he treats the people who can't do anything to further his career. I was just a young intern, but Congressman Ryun never failed to treat me with the same dignity and courtesy he offered everyone who came into his office. Not everyone was so welcoming, and the contrast was stark. One afternoon, as I walked through the tunnels underneath the Capitol, Congressman Barney Frank came barreling through a corridor, crashing into me so that I dropped what I was carrying and nearly fell over. It was only an accident, but I will not soon forget the furious glare I received at having been in his path. There are good people in Washington, but there are also a lot of decidedly unpleasant characters.

I remember watching one young volunteer eagerly pass out literature about a candidate's excellent qualifications—his rock-solid marriage, fiscal record, voting record, etc. At first I was impressed with my friend's energetic efforts to do all he could to help the candidate. Then he admitted that he was really working only because he couldn't wait to get drunk on the free booze that would be served at the campaign headquarters at the end of the evening—besides, there would be girls there.

Another acquaintance boasted to me once that he'd make a terrific candidate when he was older, because he *really was* a conservative, "not like those guys in Washington." Besides, he hadn't made many of the mistakes that would help his opponents make him look bad—just "that one orgy in the backyard that one time." A phone call interrupted his boasting. He answered and spent a few moments protesting to the woman on the line that he'd never heard of her. When she persisted, he finally admitted that he must have been drunk when they'd slept together. She was upset; he finally shouted, "Hell, I don't remember it. Was I good?" and hung up. He turned back to me and laughed—"One night and it's like they think it means something." He went back to telling me how ardently conservative he was. I couldn't help wondering, as he described his love of freedom and his wish that "those libs" would take more responsibility for their bad decisions, how he managed to justify his own actions. I didn't ask—he wouldn't have understood the question.

Drawn by the excitement generated by a popular candidate or policy, many of my peers accepted conservatism because it had been presented to them in an attractive way, not because they understood why the principles it promotes are true. Promises of "babes and beer" may help win elections and increase numbers in the short term, but they're a poor way to build up future leaders. They're also one of the most effective ways to get a young recruit's attention, especially when that recruit is ill-equipped to tackle ideas and arguments.

Organizations like the Leadership Institute, where I interned for several months, do an admirable job training young conservatives to be effective activists; however, they are necessarily limited by the quality (or lack thereof) of the education their young protégés received while growing up. There's a lot of value to the sort of training and mentorship available from places like the Leadership Institute, but it's difficult to undo the damage done by the kind of instruction most young activists receive in school.

Take my promiscuous conservative friend, for instance. He'd graduated from a good university, and he was intelligent. In a way, he was right—he had the potential to be a good candidate. He'd been well trained for the job, and his political philosophy was sound. Unfortunately, he'd been taught to assume that his moral philosophy could rightly be kept separate from his other beliefs and actions. He understood that ideas have consequences, but only partially—he didn't realize the extent to which the consequences of his ideas about morality were relevant to his political aspirations. Worse, he assumed that his personal virtue should have little to do with his career goals. He seemed to have no idea how internally fragmented he was, or how completely his education had failed to unify his beliefs. He had a good mind, but it was so enslaved to his appetites as to be almost useless to both him and to the movement he wanted to endorse.

He wasn't the first to be so fragmented, nor was he the last to let his appetites overrule his reason. That's part of why the "babes and beer" recruiting my other friend so appreciated is common—people use it because it works.

It's also part of why so many of the movement's spokesmen are stuck on the overly simplistic "Liberals are dumb" meme—it's the closest thing my generation has to a shared text. Our parents grew up with *National Review*, but we grew up with *Sesame Street*—and, as a result, radio, TV, and the Internet have had a much bigger impact on most of us than any book has. Since none of these mediums are particularly suited to the time-consuming give-and-take of a thoughtful, honest dialogue, most of us simply don't know *how* to confront an opponent's ideas fairly. It's easier to conclude, with the talk show hosts, that "liberals are dumb," and to rally the troops to action with the assumption that our nation is in constant danger of being overtaken by unthinking morons.

To be fair, I suppose some of this is to be expected. Every successful movement has—and needs—its thinkers and its doers, and these are not always the same people. Most individuals become one or the other, not both. The conservative revolution of the 1960s was unique in that it was made up of a group of people who could both think well *and* act effectively—a formidable combination. This was no accident; these leaders had to be cultivated. The Right can't rest forever on the backs of the Buckleys and Blackwells, who so successfully matched philosophy and action; if the movement is to grow and thrive in the coming years, my peers and I must learn to duplicate their integration. This much-needed balance was not an accident of earlier times, but rather the result of intentional efforts to keep ideas and actions in an appropriate tension. Future leaders must learn to cultivate this balance, but most are not very well equipped to do so.

My generation's forebears were fortunate in that their elders were willing to tell them when they were ignorant—but for our entire lives, our elders have been too busy trying to emulate us to even realize how poorly they taught us. Students are no longer given a sound grounding in the liberal arts in school, so it's no wonder they don't know how to grapple with difficult ideas properly. Like so many other young people throughout history, they fail to think through their decisions and end up fighting fiercely for something they cannot always fully define.

It doesn't have to be this way; after all, most of the very best texts in the Western canon are still readily obtainable in good English translations—thanks to the Internet, more are available than ever before. I was fortunate to discover this fact at the same time that I was learning how to be an effective activist. While working in Washington, I accepted an invitation to study at the Torrey Honors Institute, a Great Books program at Biola University. I had no idea that I'd stumbled upon one of the most rigorous classical education programs in the country—and one of academia's best-kept secrets.

Once in California, I dove into volume upon volume of Homer, Dante, Locke, Augustine, Shakespeare, and many other members of the great Western Canon. I loved my studies but was eager to get back to work in Washington—Plato and Aristotle were exhilarating and life-changing, but weren't there also elections to be won and jobs to be had? Hours spent in the library during the 2000 election left me frustrated and feisty. What was I doing locked up in an ivory tower when the future of the free world was at stake? I loved school, but I also missed the constant sense of urgency and the sort of "battle spirit" I'd felt in Washington.

My political training and my college classes didn't seem to have much in common at first. At the Leadership Institute, I gathered a lot of practical "nuts and bolts" knowledge about how to be an effective conservative activist, and at the Torrey Honors Institute, my professors were eager to teach me how to think well, how to argue fairly and effectively, how to love God and country, and how to live an upright life. I eventually discovered that not only did these two very different educational emphases complement each other beautifully, but each really *needed* the other. People who are eager to act must first learn to think well and to love the right things well. Likewise, thinkers must learn to resist the temptation to gorge themselves on knowledge without turning that knowledge into useful action.

This realization didn't always keep me from feeling restless, but halfway through college I stumbled upon a passage in Dostoevsky's *Brothers Karamazov* that made all the difference. The passage describes Alyosha, a young man who was so serious about a cause that he was willing to sacrifice his life for it; yet even with all his fervor, he was unwilling to do the hard intellectual work that would train him to think well and thus defend his cause most effectively. This describes so many young activists who are eager to represent a good cause but are unwilling to make the most important sacrifices. After a lot of thought, I decided I'd be more useful in the culture wars if I slowed down, stopped trying to get back into the election-cycle workforce, and instead spent more time trying to understand Dante's vision of Paradise, or even Hume's skepticism. This life-altering approach has always been difficult for young people, but it is especially rare now—and it is precisely the sort of long-term investment conservatives absolutely must make if they wish to have a serious impact. Conservatism would benefit tremendously if today's young activists would spend a little less time networking and a lot more time allowing the West's best foundational texts to change their lives.

Now that I'm out of college and have a family to think about, I still haven't made it back to Washington as I'd always planned—but this doesn't mean I can't have a place within the movement. To start with, I'm a mother and a homemaker, and this obviously means I have a hand in shaping the next generation. This is invaluable, but thanks to the Internet, I can also be active in more immediate ways. The digital revolution is enabling parents to keep their family life centered in the home while also earning a living, and this is good news for conservatives who want to have both a healthy family life and a larger cultural impact. For example, I edited a couple of books a few years ago, and was home to watch my daughter take her first steps while I sat working at my laptop. It made no difference to the authors or publishers that I worked on their books at my kitchen table, but it made all the difference in the world to my family. These days, I do nearly all my writing from my home. My audience can't tell the difference, and my daughter has no idea that such work is typically done in an office while the children are in daycare. She'll grow up knowing that a woman can have both a successful career *and* enjoy the traditional conservative ideals of home and family. That's as it should be, and more conservative families should take advantage of these opportunities.

They should also take advantage of the wealth of intellectual resources available to them when teaching both themselves and their children. My generation is stilsl young—we still have time to learn how to become the sort of productive, intelligent, and virtuous people whose talents and influence the conservative movement so needs, and we're certainly young enough to ensure that our children are better educated than we were. If young, politically savvy activists will revive the old shared texts and moral ideals in a winsome, open, intellectually honest way, we will be uniquely able to bring the movement into a renaissance with the power to shape not only public policy but also the future of the very Western culture we strive to protect.

12

IMMERSION EXPERIENCE

Caitrin Nicol

I was a baby revolutionary. I was not aware of it when it began, except to observe that I didn't ride the school bus, didn't have "homework," and didn't use a lunchbox—all of which seemed hopelessly glamorous by their absence. What I had instead was less tangible or easy to appreciate at the time: an organic rhythm to the day, a devoted teacher with complete creative freedom, and an infinite amount of time to read. Lincoln beautifully described writing as "the great invention of the world": "great, very great in enabling us to converse with the dead, the absent, and the unborn, at all distances of time and space." In company like that, though I was a class of one, I was not alone at all.

In the past decade, there has been an exodus from school. The National Center for Education Statistics estimates that in 2007, 1.5 million American children were educated at home—five times the number in

1990, when I didn't go to kindergarten, just a few years after the powers that be stopped sending truant officers to knock on people's doors. I like to call this wave the Revolution partly because, at a purely impressionistic level, it seems like the sort of people to whom revolutionariness is theoretically appealing are more likely to find it disturbing—there's no telling what the social conservatives are up to out of sight!—and partly because "the Revolution does Shakespeare," for instance, has a nice ring to it. (This is what my mother does these days with my younger brothers and their friends and any other homeschoolers within her gravitational pull: she directs them in full-blown productions of Shakespeare plays. Practicing a scene is an opportunity to talk about the characters, the tension, the context, the words; going over lines is an opportunity to imprint stretches of the greatest English ever written on the memory for good. I mention this as an example of the way that the new outré educators handle the responsibility of teaching.)

Parents choose to homeschool for any number of reasons. Mine kept me home because there are not enough hours in the day to justify parking a young child at a desk inside a room for mind-boggling amounts of time when there are so many other things to do. For every reason to homeschool, there is a chorus faithfully protesting it, and like most controversies in education policy, it is not actually *about* education policy. The most common concern by far is socialization, which as often as not has a political angle. This anxiety is nicely summed up by an op-ed that a commentator by the name of M. J. Andersen published in the local paper when I was in eighth grade, which, with equal parts bathos and condescension, pleaded with conservatives to keep their kids in school. At the time, it got my friends and me all riled up, and we dashed off an outraged letter to the editor about all the different people that we knew; now, however, I am more inclined to find it rather droll: "There these kids will be," she wrote, "never knowing what it is to sit next to the one who smells, or wears ugly shoes; the one who runs like the wind but cannot add, and cries in defeat; the one with the funny accent; the one whose skin is darker or lighter; whose hair is silkier, or coarser, or teased high; the child who has more; who has less; who never speaks of home, because it is a sad and secret place. The public schools offer enough of an education in democracy to break your heart. They may be the only true civic training many of us will ever get. So what happens when hordes of children desert, and grow up unable to imagine anyone unlike themselves?"

It will be a sorry day when civic life is mediated wholly through the public schools, but this fear is born more of a failure of imagination on Ms. Andersen's part than of reality. In point of fact, though, her unstated premise is quite right: we only really learn who people are by personal interaction. For this reason, it seems clear that she has never met real live homeschoolers, or perhaps she would know better. Certainly, where I grew up, different kinds of people living on the same land seemed to track on different orbits—or, more accurately, inhabit parallel universes. There was the general community, whose pulse was set by the Ivy League university where my father worked, and there was our invisible counterculture.

And though the habits of the counterculture were never as regressive as its critics like to think, set that aside and imagine for a moment that it was just as spooky as you please, because that makes the next part more interesting: in ninth grade, I crossed over and enrolled in public school, at an institution philosophically located on the outer reaches of the Left.

I liked school; strangely enough, it felt like summer camp to me, being part of an entire herd of kids steered from one activity to the next. But the politics—the politics were everywhere, and were like a person loudly talking to himself. There were no counterpoints and no one to convince, simply a gong to bang for the spiritual satisfaction of it, or perhaps to ward off evil energy from the Right. I was uncertain of my own views on most issues at the time, but while I thought them through, it troubled me that the sinister intent of people I knew at least a little bit about was universally assumed. I felt it was incumbent on me, as the sole emissary from an alien land, to put together a better public relations package.

This burden was dragging around with me when, one fine afternoon, I approached the bus stop where a classmate I somewhat knew and another I had never seen before were chattering away about abortion politics. I have no idea why two fifteen-year-old guys were sitting under a tree talking about that, or why I thought it was the opening I had been waiting for, but, announcing myself, I was instantly snowed under as my classmate leaped to his feet and unleashed an avalanche of thought. His friend evaporated, while he and I continued the discussion on the bus and later via e-mail. Over the next week, we worked our way through the meaning of history, whether truth is absolute or relative, the question of evil, and other matters well within our ken. I was lost. Worse, I felt that I was mangling important ideas that deserved a better voice, so, with a melodramatic flourish, I shut down the conversation.

Sam—that was his name (not really)—was a geyser of opinions and orations and ideas, who rambled around perpetually disheveled by sheer force of cerebral energy. He had a charmingly kooky demeanor, a big heart for everyone around him, an even worse sense of direction than I did, and a singing voice on loan from God. But I would not find this out for a long time, because I was so embarrassed that I totally avoided him. Meanwhile, however, I determined to do one thing: I would return to the issue of abortion, do some research, marshal my thoughts, and write a defense of life.

As it happened, there was a statewide speech contest on the Constitution that my U.S. history teacher was interested in sponsoring. A fellow traveler of Howard Zinn, she was a charismatic Texan earth mother who had us call her simply Marla and taught us how the Man done wrong. Her second-favorite mantra was "you bought the lie"—but her first was "use your voice," and it was an idea she absolutely stood behind. There is a maxim attributed (erroneously) to Voltaire: "I disapprove of what you say, but I will defend to the death your right to say it." You have probably heard people say this before, and probably thought that they were full of it. Marla, however, spent untold afternoons helping me write and practice this anti-*Roe* speech, and drove me up and down the state to deliver it. She watched me speak with a look on her face like she wished she could believe in a world where that was her position, too.

Marla presided over a cult following of the most politically passionate students, whom she eventually assembled into a debate squad. Uninterested in standard-variety high school debauchery, these were the driven radicals, itching to do battle with all the imperfections of the world—and too absorbed in their own causes to take part in the casual corrosive attitude endemic to the rest of the school. Though the substance of their convictions was foreign to me, the intensity was familiar: they were kindred spirits through the looking-glass. A shy little intergalactic migrant, I had the pleasure of being welcomed into their open moon-bat arms.

The first to befriend me was Luke, a merry six-foot-plus impresario who could strike up a conversation with a hole in the wall. A hugger of trees, he was devoted to Ralph Nader, and liked to beat that drum in no small part to get a rise out of people who were existentially afraid that Nader would hand over the 2000 election to George W. Bush. "Vote your conscience," was Luke's beatific rejoinder. The mysteries of conscience were endlessly amusing to him, not because they were trivial but because, as I once heard somewhere, if we cannot laugh at what is sacred then we cannot laugh at anything—for what isn't sacred? He was in my biology class, and any time the lecture ventured near such topics as "fossil record" or "natural selection," he would begin bouncing up and down, turn to me with a Cheshire grin, and devilishly cock an eyebrow. He found this routine so hilarious that I didn't have the heart to tell him I was not the creationist that he supposed.

(Unrelatedly, I have never been to Luke's house at any hour of day or night when there was not a pot of ramen noodles bubbling on the stove. I eventually came to believe that this is a spiritual ritual for the family, an ongoing offering to a parochial noodle deity who diligently protects the household from becoming more normal than it is. I like to imagine they arrange their ramen duties by ship's bell: "Joey, 03:00. Your watch.")

Luke's best friend, Daniel, was a white-hot flame of pacifism. He agonized about sanctions and no-fly zones and occupation and the works. In debate scrimmages, he spoke like the fate of the human race depended on what happened in the round. When U.S. forces invaded Afghanistan and then Iraq, he and Luke and company stood day after day in several feet of snow (always in Birkies, with or without socks), waving cardboard signs and trying to communicate to passing cars that war is horrifying. For whose benefit, exactly? We're talking about rural New England roads with a few stray vehicles, whose drivers would reliably be anti-Bush already. This bordered on the absurd—but just as Luke saw comedy in the sacrosanct, there was something sanctified about this comedy.

Daniel was lit from within by deep moral instincts that were not mine. This is an unremarkable circumstance that becomes dizzying when you try to stare at it directly. What is the meaning of our beliefs, which come from outside ourselves, and point us beyond ourselves, but seemingly do not derive from the same source or point in the same direction?

It is tempting to relativize them, and easy enough for anybody who does not have firm convictions of his own; but this is to say that they mean almost nothing. This position has its very own decal: the stupendously annoying "Coexist" bumper sticker, in which each letter takes the form of a different religious or political symbol. Its sole purpose is to broadcast the moral superiority of people not confined to a particular tradition in the first place, and does less than nothing to further actual coexistence, as desirable as that may be.

Another popular approach is to dispatch the ideas that one doesn't share or understand as either disingenuous or delusional. But apart from all the obvious problems with that, it bankrupts the strength of character in people—and what could be more dear, or less replaceable?

I support the U.S. military's efforts in the war on terror, not because the collateral damage does not matter but because of what is at stake. (No one, after all, believes in war for its own sake.) And yet, our national conscience depends in part on people like Daniel, to whom the larger picture is *not* as important as the individual lives being lost—because to the bereaved, these losses are not "in perspective," either. They are everything. And we would be a callous people if some of us did not mourn them as though they really are.

That is a policy example of a question that runs much deeper than policy. But it was a way to begin thinking about it. As for Daniel, he grew into his vocation and found himself a larger audience. For the past few years, he worked for a Palestinian news agency in the West Bank, until—for reasons that remain unclear—he was detained by Israeli authorities for several days at Ben Gurion Airport, repeatedly interrogated, and in the end deported back to the United States. "Most Likely to Be Involved in an International Incident" was not in our yearbook, but in a strange way it seems to me that he would not be fulfilling his potential if he *weren't* doing something that came at a cost.

These were some of the people I most admired in my sojourn on the Left—Daniel with his peace on earth, Luke with his goodwill toward men, and Marla, the best kind of teacher. Also Sam, whom Marla had assigned to be my debate partner. I was none too thrilled, because that meant I actually had to talk to him, awkwardness and all. Sam, who was too kind ever to reproach me afterward, had an insatiable interest in everything—and what had been confusing before became exhilarating. Politics was only the smallest and least heady part. We would go to tournaments in strange cities, invariably get lost, and, like Shakespeare's great old king, "take upon us the mystery of things as if we were God's spies" while wandering around in the rain. The one time he ever struggled to find words was when I fell in love with him and he had to tell me that he was gay. That afternoon, all the songs and arguments and big ideas and vistas were dissolved, leaving only two kids trying not to break each other's hearts.

It dawned on me years after the fact that this is what the op-ed writer chiefly had in mind when she worried about Right-wing homeschoolers encountering "anyone unlike themselves." The hope is that exposure to "diversity," as defined by various agendas, instills a kind of comprehensive sympathy where there was none before. The trouble with that line of thinking is that it treats people as if they exist only to belong to categories—and when you actually care for someone, the categories are what matter least about him.

Nonetheless, people organize themselves by labels well enough for there to be a sharp cultural divide, and there is a great deal of mutual suspicion being harbored in the trenches. Maybe it is equally distributed and maybe not, but that's beside the point. Good people, disgusted by the vitriol, look for salvation in leaders' perennial odes to bipartisanship, but that is also not the point. Political cooperation cannot paper over the apparently irreconcilable worldviews at the heart of who we are. And while there is no shortcut for the seekers—parallel lines converge at infinity; what of parallel universes?—we live in a marvelous, improbable, preposterous nation that stakes its ideals around the opportunity to seek. I would only note that "seek and ye shall find" is a two-Testament promise; it is also the underlying premise of the scientific method and of rational philosophy. In that, there is a crazy kind of hope for anyone who wants to come on out and parley.

Meanwhile, the country and its ideals will not seem worth defending to people who are busy raining bile on each other's consciences. Loving America means loving Americans, in all of their bewildering variety, not as abstract categories but face by face by face.

13

CONFESSIONS OF A RADICAL REPUBLICAN

Matt Patterson

What makes someone a conservative? A liberal? The subject fascinates me, not least because the words are so slippery and amorphous. They change meaning from one era to another and, indeed, from one person to another.

My voting habits would seem to place me in the "conservative" camp of the contemporary, bifurcated American political scene. I find this irredeemably amusing, because I am not a conservative. I *am*, however, a republican, and a Republican.

My allegiance is first to the republican ideal, then to our particular and peculiar American Republic, and last to the Republican Party. And my loyalty to the last two endures in direct correlation to their fidelity to the first.

The word *republic* comes to us from the Ancient Roman *res publica*—literally, "public thing"—and commonly denotes any popular form of government. More specifically, however, a republic represents a brilliant compromise between two classes that have ever been in conflict, a power-sharing arrangement between plebs and patricians. When the former alone rule, you have pure democracy; when the latter, oligarchy; both are equally deleterious to liberty.

Republics strike a harmonious balance between the two extremes, an equilibrium almost magically conducive to the institution, preservation, and expansion of individual freedom. This is why republican principles and republican institutions are worthy of life, love, and loyalty.

I was attracted to republicanism (and the Republican Party, thanks to Ronald Reagan) from an early age. But it wasn't until I became a young man that I met someone who showed me firsthand how those principles can improve the lives of individual people; how liberty, opportunity, and ambition can conspire to ignite the fires of prosperity.

His name was Mario Padrino.

The man looked at me, then cocked his head. "Well," he began.

No. Not again. I had been coming into Padrino's Restaurant in Plantation, Florida, every week for at least a year, making my case and hearing the same response every time. The same response I was hearing now.

"I don't know," Mario Padrino, owner and manager, continued. He stood, one hand up to his chin, one folded across his chest. And smiling, always smiling.

"Look," I said in the lobby of his beautiful bistro. "I'll be here tomorrow at seven. We'll try it, no charge, and see how it goes." I shook his hand and before he could respond, turned and exited into the moist curtain of South Florida air.

I figured one of two things would happen when I arrived the next night: either Mario would let me do my thing, or I would be forcibly ejected (and possibly arrested). I decided to risk it.

My "thing" was (and still is, in some sultry corner of my soul, now seldom visited) close-up magic. Close-up is a curious subspecies of theatrical entertainment; forgoing the stage and its trappings, the close-up performer entertains in intimate settings with items small enough to be secreted in the pocket—playing cards, coins, rope, and the like.

These magicians have one great advantage over their stage-bound brethren in the wide variety of workable venues available to them. Any place where people gather, standing or seated, is a natural habitat for the enterprising close-up artist—dinners, cocktail parties, picnics, etc.; these sorts of private engagements make up the bulk of the close-up artist's income. But you need to advertise, and the best way to do that is to perform regularly in a busy restaurant, like Padrino's, where every table is like a mini-audition.

Close-up, being a rather exotic form of entertainment, is a tough sell for any restaurant manager, but Mario Padrino was an especially interesting challenge. After coming in and making my pitch to him so often, I could tell that he was not opposed to restaurant magic in theory (and that he perhaps harbored some affection for the art generally), but that he nonetheless had some reservations—no pun intended—about how the process would work in his establishment: Would I be a bother to his customers? Would I get in the way of his staff? Was I any *good*?

I decided I was just going to have to show him.

The next night, I showed up and, to my delight, was allowed to start performing. Mario followed, carefully watching me interact with his guests. Every now and again I would steal a glance backward to gauge his reaction, but his mustachioed visage was implacably impassive.

Eventually Mario stopped following me, and I saw him speaking at length with customers for whom I had already performed. Finally he abandoned even that, and went about his normal business, leaving me to perform for whomever I saw fit for as long as they desired.

At the end of the night, he approached me, smiling, and shook my hand. "See you tomorrow?" I asked.

He laughed. "Sure," he said, "but we're still on trial." Right, I said, and walked out.

I came back the next night. And the weekend after that. I gave him a couple more nights free—ordinarily I wouldn't do that more than once, for fear of an unscrupulous manager taking advantage of some free entertainment. But I trusted Mario, and sure enough, it wasn't long before he started paying me, though I don't recall him ever saying the words *you're hired.* I just kept showing up, and he kept paying me. Eventually he asked me to perform at more of his restaurants, and on occasion even to entertain guests at private functions at his home.

Over the ensuing years, my muse often took me out of state, around the country, and across the globe. But when in Florida, I always had a place to perform at Padrino's, and was glad for it: being a freelance entertainer—or a freelance anything—means whiplash swings between times of plenty and paucity, and my gigs at Mario's restaurants provided a blessed buffer from these vagaries. But in the end, I got more out of the experience than mere change in my pocket and food in my belly—I gained an invaluable example.

You see, at the end of the night, Mario and I would often chat in his office. He had all of these motivational posters up on his wall, business-oriented self-help mottoes and such. He loved to talk about business theory and practice, the nature of success, and how these principles could be applied to my career as a magician. I listened; I had been a starving artist and found no romance in the beast.

Years later, I was visiting friends up north. As we were driving home from dinner, a woman running a red light plowed into us. Our car spun around and almost went into a storefront. When we came to a stop, I hopped out—at first everyone seemed okay, but then I looked down and noticed: my left arm was twisted 'round like a pretzel.

As I was wheeled in surgery that night, I told someone (the doctor? a nurse?) that I had to be out by Friday because I had U2 tickets. I was informed without sentiment that not only would I miss the show but I would be lucky to have my arm when I woke up.

My arm was still attached when I came to, though buried under mountains of gauze and plaster. The accident had shattered my left humerus into a dozen pieces. In addition, nerves and tissue running the length of my arm had sustained serious trauma. I was all but crippled.

Recovery took multiple surgeries and many excruciating years. I was forced to contemplate the possibility that my magic career was over for good, a thought that plunged me into the blackest depression.

I'm not quite sure why, but at some point in my convalescence it occurred to me to write a book for magicians. What was then sorely lacking in the magic literature, as far as I knew, were solid business manuals that dispensed practical advice on how to make a living at close-up. Since my career might be over, I reasoned, why not try and help someone else make a go of it?

I began to think about the kind of book that would have benefited me when I had started. I wrote that book as best I could (a lot of one-handed typing), printed it, advertised it, sold it. It did pretty well for a first-time, self-published effort, receiving excellent reviews from the major trade publications. My career as a magician was over; my career as a writer had begun.

It was only later that I realized how much of the business acumen that I had acquired and then channeled into my book (both into the text and into the enterprise of selling it) had arisen from my conversations with Mario. In retrospect, I should have thanked him in the acknowledgments. He was in there, just the same; the cover featured a photo of myself entertaining a table of patrons—at Padrino's.

But business is not all I learned from Mario. Equally fascinating to me was his family's story, their removal from Castro's Cuba and subsequent coming to, and prospering in, the United States. Mario could extol the virtues of America better than any politician I had ever heard.

I don't remember Mario's politics. If he told me how he voted, I don't remember, and wouldn't say anyhow. But, to me, his message was a profoundly conservative one.

Or so it seemed at the time.

My republicanism often puts me at odds with what is commonly called "conservatism." Take, as but one example, our imbecilic and tyrannical drug war, supported largely by conservative political forces. Why is it any of the government's business what a grown person puts into his or her body? You may say that narcotic use is immoral and irresponsible. Perhaps. But what is freedom if not the freedom to be those things? Good only matters as a choice if bad exists as an option, something God surely knew when he created Lucifer.

I speak in the last metaphorically, of course, which leads to another area of demarcation between myself and modern conservatism: I eschew religion.

I know that some sects of protestantism have contributed significantly to the formation and evolution of capitalism, and am grateful for it. And I am proud to count many Christians as both political allies and personal friends. But the self-immolation required by the major faiths offends my deepest republican predilections. Lucifer, in fact, should surely be a republican saint for his refusal to bow before a monarch, even (especially) a celestial one.

As for our earthly messiah, give me Lincoln over Jesus. I *know* Lincoln existed—I need no faith. I see his legacy with my own eyes; I live in his handiwork, and have seen his physical remains, his tomb, clothes, hat; indeed, his blood and hair are on public display for anyone to see. A race of men once enslaved but now free; an intact nation into which I was born and have prospered. These are Lincoln's works—republican works.

In a republic, plebs and patricians each have a hand on the reins of state. Our Founders were aware of the sagacity of this arrangement—they enshrined it in our own Constitution, in the People's House and its legislative coconspirator, the austere and aristocratic Senate, as well as in a chief executive whose power comes directly from the people and not from the blessing of God or purse or blood but is nonetheless electorally shielded from the passions of the public for four-year intervals.

Let us be blunt, shall we? Historically, these kinds of states are rare and fragile creatures, found in only a few anomalous locales and eras. Indeed, the idea that the common man should have a say in his own governance must be ranked among the most bizarre and radical notions ever to have occurred to Man—certainly, the vast multitude who have ever gathered themselves into civilizations have done so under one form of tyranny or another.

Tyranny, not liberty, seems to be the natural order, on Earth as in Heaven. In *Escape from Freedom*, Erich Fromm offers a diagnosis for this chronic human condition. The myriad choices that freedom offers is a source of deep spiritual anxiety, says Fromm, causing our "fear of freedom" and all-too-often flight into the restricting but comforting arms of the state.

Our modern world is no different. Statism continues to exert a powerful and comforting pall over many of the earth's peoples, and the republican ideal is as radical and rare as ever.

If the republican ideal is radical, then the political party that bears the name is equally so. What I have always loved about the Republican Party, in fact, is its radical nature. In its infancy, it was unalterably opposed to the *ancien regime* of human bondage, and consecrated itself to the restriction and then destruction of the "barbarity" of slavery.

Today, the Republican Party is dedicated—however imperfectly—to slowing, obstructing, halting the creep of government into every aspect of our lives. This indeed has been the constant thread running right through the century-and-a-half history of the party—the promotion and expansion of individual liberty.

This is precisely why I fear for my party, my country, and the republican ideal, for there are weaknesses, perhaps fatal weaknesses, inherent in republicanism and the free markets that sustain it, weaknesses that are seldom addressed or even understood by modern "conservatives," who are the ostensible defenders of the faith.

Republicans and conservatives are fond of saying that their preferred system removes government as an obstacle, allowing people to pursue their dreams unfettered. All too true—which is why many are terrified of it.

Because the harsh truth is this—not everyone will or can achieve their dreams. It is the nature of dreams, in fact, that they are unattainable to all but the most talented, fierce, and determined. And even many of these hardy souls will need luck, mentors (like Mario), family; some form of support and encouragement along the way. Not all will get it.

In short, there is no guarantee of anything, for anyone, in a republic, save freedom. But that is not enough: people *want* a guarantee—often more, it seems, than they want freedom.

This is why, for most people in most times, the blanket of government has proven a welcome succor; it both shields them from the worst vicissitudes of the state of nature and assures that, even if they can't rise as high as they want, they will never sink so low as they fear. The pangs of excellence exchanged for the pangs of failure—for many, a fine bargain.

Unfree ideologies are fiercely competitive in the marketplace of ideas because they appeal to and generally cohere via an alliance of two crucial constituencies:

1. Those unable to achieve on their own, and therefore grateful and greedy for government tit upon which to suckle.
2. Those of privilege, who have trappings of success but through no effort of their own, and so lash out at the system that produces wealth and reminds them of their own parasitic nature.

What the two have in common is both a loathing for, and fear of, freedom and its terrible possibilities. Between them, a Faustian bargain is often struck; people and princes decide together to accrue power to the princes alone, and in return for taking sole control, the princes offer the people payments in government monies.

This is how republics die.

Conservatives have never fully understood, nor sympathized with, this entirely legitimate fear of freedom. And so the Left's promises of government-provided security, and its honeyed lies that everyone is the same and that therefore those who have more must have ill-gotten their riches, will continue to resonate with a large and restless contingent.

How can we possibly compete with this in the long term? Jealousy. Failure. Fear. These will ever be present in the human heart, and will always drive the wretched into the arms of the state (or the church), to smooth over inequity both material and celestial, and there will always be a governing elite, a princely class, all-too-happy to oblige.

We on the Right must reexamine our most cherished belief that, without government, everyone can rise and flourish. Because this isn't true. Some people, many people, perhaps most people, *will* be better off with government largesse, and they know it. And what can we say to that? Are we "conservatives" and Republicans willing to confront this reality?

Mario Padrino was an inspiration to me. A conservative one, I thought. But the more I have studied the history of our species, and the geography of the human heart, the more I have recognized his example to be both radical and rare, like some exotic flower wavering in an unstable, evanescent oasis.

The United States was such an oasis. But, starting in the twentieth century, the waters of our liberty began to evaporate, and the sands of statism began to creep in. The New Deal, the Great Society—grand names for grand schemes to desiccate our republican institutions.

And now, at the dawn of this new century, the sun beats down with renewed brutality as the forces of unfreedom press their advantage: government-managed health care; government control of a naturally occurring by-product of life and work, carbon dioxide—consummation of these long-held liberal lusts spells the end of freedom.

Our American Republic, like its great ancestor long dead by Caesar's sword, will sooner or later seem another mirage of history, a place where people and princes once ruled together for the liberty of both. And the men and women who created and sustained it will be remembered for what they were:

Radicals. Not conservatives.

14

A "FRANK" EXCHANGE

The Tale of My Political Conversion

Joel B. Pollak

When my wife (then fiancée), Julia, and I heard that Rep. Barney Frank (D-MA) would be coming to Harvard University's Kennedy School of Government in April 2009 to give an address about the ongoing financial crisis, we immediately made plans to attend.

We were both in our final year at Harvard—she at the college, I at the law school—and busy enough with our search for jobs without spending yet another evening on politics. Yet we jumped at the chance to challenge the congressman who had blocked attempts to regulate Fannie Mae and Freddie Mac, chief culprits in the subprime mortgage crisis.

My wife, who studied economics, had prepared a question about financial markets. I wanted to challenge the hypocrisy of Rep. Frank's attack on corporate bonuses, when congressional staffers had just earned a bonus for 2008. As I listened to his speech and heard his response to the first few questions from the floor, I was struck at how breezily he blamed everyone else for the crisis. Not content with blaming George W. Bush, Rep. Frank tried to implicate every conservative from Ronald Reagan in the 1980s all the way back to Robert Taft in the 1930s. A new question formed in my mind as I stepped to the microphone.

"How much responsibility, if any, do you have for the financial crisis?" I asked.

Rep. Frank lost his temper, labeling me as part of a "Right-wing attack" and avoiding an answer. So I do what young lawyers are taught to do when facing a hostile witness: repeat the question.

That outraged him even more, but I kept my cool. My wife did not. "Stop labeling him!" she yelled at Rep. Frank. "I like labels," he snapped back.

Our exchange continued for a few more minutes before the dean of the school called proceedings to an abrupt and early end. I went back to the library, expecting that my standoff with Rep. Frank might merit a mention in the next morning's *Harvard Crimson*, if that. Little did I know that the local Fox News affiliate had taped the debate and posted it online. Soon it was on YouTube, being watched by thousands. It was featured by both Fox and MSNBC, the Right- and Left-wing networks finding rare agreement in their judgment that Rep. Frank had behaved boorishly. I was on several television and radio shows, and received e-mails and letters from around the country. Soon afterward, several Republicans back home in Illinois encouraged me to run for Congress in my home district.

Five months later, I decided to go for it.

I had traveled a long political journey since I first arrived at Harvard as a college freshman in 1995, a public-school kid nurtured on romantic histories of the civil rights movement and the antiwar protests of the 1960s. I believed that the role of government was to rearrange society in order to help the poor and disadvantaged. My classmates and professors tended to hold similar views, which reinforced mine.

I felt a sense of restless impatience about the world, which reflected my beliefs. I studied with Cornel West, then Harvard's superstar in Afro-American studies. My final paper was titled "Communitarianism and the Redress of Racial and Class Injustice." In it, I proposed "a system of communal, public boarding schools," and "creating new jobs in federally subsidized industries," among other radical ideas. I chose to enter the Social Studies program, an application-only concentration in which students were drilled in the basics of social and political theory, most of it Left-wing. I took more Cornel West, this time writing about "transformative communication" and suggesting "public or cooperative ownership of the communicative media." I helped organize a campus "teach-in." I interned for Left-wing politicians and organizations.

In 1996, I cast my first-ever presidential vote for Ralph Nader, writing his name in on my Illinois ballot. I grew my hair long, into a giant blond "Jewfro"—the way many of my classmates at Harvard still remember me. I was a radical—albeit an increasingly frustrated one, as I wrestled with the obvious contradictions between what I was being taught in class and what I observed in the "real world."

In my junior year, I added Environmental Science & Public Policy as a second concentration—much to the frustration of the Harvard administration, since no one had combined my two fields before. It was then that my first conservative impulses began. I was alarmed at the degree to which environmental scientists aspired to change—and control—individual choices in order to achieve ecological utopia. Our professors would admit, for example, that we did not quite understand how the warming effect of carbon dioxide and other "greenhouse gases" might be offset by the cooling effect of aerosols in the atmosphere, or that our most sophisticated computer models still could not tell us the precise effects on climate of increased average surface temperatures. Yet they had no problem supporting sweeping changes to our economy, whose costs were certain and whose benefits were unclear.

I remember writing—without much sense of irony—a term paper about how Galileo might have approached the climate-change debate. My suggestion was that contemporary scientists write dramatic dialogues to convince the public of the reality of climate change, much as Galileo had written dialogues about the earth revolving around the sun. It somehow escaped me that Galileo was persecuted precisely because his views stood apart from the "consensus" of the day.

Eventually, the restlessness provoked by these contradictions began to overtake me. It was the hypocrisy of many Left-wing icons that first inspired me to shake loose. When Michael Moore gave a lecture at the Kennedy School in the fall of 1997 about his film *The Big One*, which focused on the plight of low-wage workers, I asked him—in front of a packed audience—whether he had paid the interns who had worked on the film. He admitted, to murmurs of disapproval from a hitherto adoring crowd, that he had not.

I began to attend conservative lectures—not because I agreed with the speakers but because I enjoyed asking tough questions without being told I was motivated by unconscious prejudicial assumptions. I did thesis research in northern Alaska, and discovered indigenous communities that regarded oil development as a boon, not a threat. I still identified as "Left-wing," but felt increasingly ill at ease with what I was supposed to believe.

In 2000, I headed to South Africa as a Rotary Ambassadorial Scholar. I was born in Johannesburg in 1977, then carried to the USA a few weeks later—so the fellowship was, in a sense, a return to my roots. But it was also a chance for me to study South Africa's democratic experiment closely. I was enthralled not only by its transition to democracy but also by the new government's avowedly Left-wing policies and ethos.

As I arrived, President Thabo Mbeki launched his campaign against the theory that HIV causes AIDS. I began tutoring high school students in Khayelitsha, one of the poorest areas in Cape Town, and learned that schools in black communities were worse after apartheid than before. Centralized planning by the national government and redistribution of resources from rich to poor districts had not improved results.

The few people I met who were managing to prosper in the midst of extreme poverty were those who had started their own businesses. Typically, they had done so with no help from the government. They saw politicians and police as obstacles to their success. Poverty continued to fester all around, with the national government claiming sole power to change circumstances and then failing utterly to do so.

What had the most profound effect on me, however, was a confrontation that I had with South African cabinet minister Ronnie Kasrils. Kasrils had launched a petition in October 2001, in the name of "South Africans of Jewish Descent," which blamed Israel for the second intifada. In the wake of 9/11 and the awful World Conference Against Racism in Durban, South African Jews reacted angrily to Kasrils's effort.

I found myself caught in the middle. I had rented a room with a Muslim family in a Muslim area—partly out of economic necessity, party out of cultural curiosity. I was also involved with the Jewish community, leading Orthodox services at a local congregation. I tried to convince Kasrils to change his declaration, then feuded with him publicly as he persisted with his attacks on Israel and the Jewish community.

What alarmed me most about the debate was the willful ignorance of the facts among Kasrils and his supporters. To the far Left, truth and right did not matter. What defined morality was the perceived position of each side within a global system. Though outnumbered by its enemies, Israel was a strong military ally of the United States and therefore could do no right, just as the Palestinians could do no wrong.

I was contemplating a return to the USA or a new adventure elsewhere when I received a call from the office of the leader of South Africa's "official" opposition party, Tony Leon. Tony had seen a few of my articles in local papers—notably, an op-ed in which I applied two months of research to explaining the differences between South Africa's negotiated democracy and the Israeli-Palestinian peace process.

I was offered a job as Tony's speechwriter, and I accepted immediately. What better way to learn about South Africa's fascinating new democracy than to experience it firsthand? As I churned out speeches and articles from my small office in the South African parliament, and watched the battle of ideas and tactics on the floor of the National Assembly, my views on politics and public policy began to crystallize.

Tony's party, the Democratic Alliance, stood for free markets, civil liberties, and the rule of law and the constitution. In American terms, it would be roughly equivalent to Bill Clinton's New Democrats or to Reagan's Republicans without the component of social conservatism (though the party's base was predominantly Christian, it did not take formal positions on abortion, gay marriage, or the death penalty).

Tony believed strongly in two ideas in particular. One was opposition to collective guilt. It was true that whites in general had benefited from apartheid at the expense of blacks. But not every white South African had been a perpetrator, and not every black South African had been a victim. Without a strong notion of individual justice, there would be no end to collective retribution, no forgiveness, and no progress. The other idea was constitutionalism—or, more precisely, the checks on majority power that South Africa's constitution provided. In principle, South Africa's constitution created several institutions intended to restrain the power of the ruling majority in parliament. In practice, the ruling majority simply appointed its own members to head those institutions. Watching Tony defend his ideas against overwhelming political odds was an inspiration.

When I returned to the United States, I still thought of myself as a Democrat. I had never voted Republican, though I had been strongly tempted to do so in 2004 and I knew that my views on the economy and the war on terror more closely matched those of the GOP. I enrolled in Harvard Law School and was elected in my first year to be my section's representative to the school's Democrat-affiliated organization.

I realized right away that I had little in common with my fellow Democrats. Either I had changed during my time abroad, or the party had shifted radically Leftward in the time I was away—or both. Regardless, we were often at odds. On one occasion, when I was arguing against a hasty withdrawal from Iraq and for the need to send more troops, a friend looked at me and asked: "Are you sure you're a Democrat?"

I can remember the moment I knew that I wasn't. I was in my civil procedure class, sitting in the back row, watching my classmates watch late results from the 2006 midterm elections on their laptops as we all pretended to take notes. I remember the excitement that swept the room when the *New York Times* Web site announced that the Democrats had, in fact, won control of the Senate. I was dismayed. Nancy Pelosi and her crew, I felt, stood for nothing. They had no ideas, no policy alternatives, except rabid hostility to George W. Bush. My father, a man of staunchly independent temperament, advised me to wait and see what the new Democrat majority would accomplish. I predicted they would accomplish exactly nothing—not even for their most devoted followers, seeking merely to score political points for two years.

I wandered in the wilderness of political independence for a year or so. I entertained the idea of writing speeches for Barack Obama, whom I imagined as an independent political spirit from my home state. I began to question such thoughts after reading his second book, *The Audacity of Hope*, and finding it a profound disappointment. He could articulate both sides of every issue, but invariably chose the wrong one. Meanwhile, I marveled at the popularity of Left-wing ideas at the law school. People were less interested in the law itself than in what the law could be used to do, in an activist sense. Few were skeptical about the role of government—partly because many planned to run it. I took comfort in the classics, which I studied with Harvey Mansfield at the College—making up for what I had missed as an undergraduate.

I did not take the final step of becoming a Republican for quite some time. I was hampered by my Democrat past and by the stigma that haunts any party that champions the right of individuals to succeed, and the right of successful individuals to keep more of what they have. To be Republican, in the imagination of urban popular culture, is to be rich, white, and male—and to be suspected of the concomitant sins of greed, racism, and sexism.

I found an unlikely figure leading me to the GOP: John McCain. I had long admired him, even when I was a Democrat, for what I perceived as his political courage, his ability to say and do what was right even when it was not what was popular. After the election, it seemed clear to many Republicans that McCain's potential to attract Democrats, as a moderate, had been an illusion. I suppose I was one of the few, then.

But it wasn't McCain's moderation that drew me to him as a candidate, and to the Republican Party as a new political home. It was his support for the surge in Iraq, the additional twenty thousand troops deployed in 2007 to reinforce coalition forces and ultimately to rout al-Qaeda. McCain defended his views when even Republicans who had supported the war were backing away from it. I respected that, and agreed.

Once I decided to support McCain, and to volunteer for him—lending my efforts as a volunteer speechwriter for the national campaign and going door-to-door in New Hampshire—I allowed myself to embrace openly the Republican Party itself. The feeling was one of relief. Once I got over the reaction of my peers—"You're the first Republican I've ever met," was a typical response at Harvard—the rest was easy. Gone were the restlessness and self-doubt I had felt as a Democrat, and which I believe many of my friends on the Left still feel. My political beliefs no longer felt at odds with the realities of the world around me. And I did away with the nagging, debilitating sense of guilt that accompanies Left-wing politics in general, which, in my experience, functions as more of a faith movement than the supposedly religious Right.

My wife traveled the same road with me. We had met in Tony Leon's office, where she had been working for a few months before enrolling as a Harvard undergraduate—an intern romance with a happy ending!

Her mother, Rhoda Kadalie, had been one of South Africa's foremost antiapartheid activists and had been appointed by Nelson Mandela to the country's Human Rights Commission. She later resigned in protest against the ruling party's refusal to investigate its own shortcomings. Julia's great-grandfather, Clements Kadalie, had been the first black trade-unionist in Africa. It was a long legacy of activism whose enduring theme was the importance of principle over partisanship. I followed Julia back to Harvard, where we cultivated a romance that was also an intertwining of political ideas and religious faith. We went door-to-door together for the McCain-Palin ticket in the countryside of New Hampshire, where we were greeted with relief by residents hitherto besieged by Obama canvassers. Our work together in that lost but worthy cause cemented our shared political commitments.

Once I became open about my political loyalties in that 2008 election—Sarah Palin button and all—I found myself becoming more open about other beliefs as well. I had long been keeping the Jewish Sabbath, keeping a kosher home, and putting on tefillin in the mornings when I could manage the time. I began wearing a yarmulke as well, an outward sign of faith and identity. I felt at peace with myself in general.

What I was not happy about was the result of the 2008 election and its aftermath. I saw in Barack Obama's presidency the roots of a cult of personality. I recognized in the Democrats' eager rush to consolidate political power, and to expand rapidly the role of the federal government in the American economy—a dangerous majoritarian impulse that our Constitution, and my experience in South Africa, warned against. Immediately after the election ended, I began writing down my thoughts about what had happened, and what it meant for the future of the United States and the world. The result of my efforts, which continued throughout the bitterly cold winter, was a book called *Don't Tell*

Me Words Don't Matter: How Rhetoric Won the 2008 Presidential Election.

In the summer of 2009, I took the book on a tour around the country, just as town hall meetings were erupting in protest at the Democrats' health care reform bill. The legislation sought to overhaul one-sixth of the nation's economy, at a cost of well over a trillion dollars, accompanied by a new federal bureaucracy that would intrude into life-and-death decisions made between doctors and their patients. Americans suspected—quite rightly—that the bill was a "Trojan horse" to impose a "single-payer" system of socialized medicine. That, in turn, would be the gateway to other radical changes, designed to maximize Democrat control of the levers of power under the guise of social justice. In the wake of a bloated "stimulus" bill and a cap-and-trade bill that would damage American industry, it sparked an uprising.

In my travels, I spoke to hundreds of people who were outraged at the direction the country was moving in, and who shared a sense of urgency about the need to restore a balance in American politics. As the health care battle dragged on, and the deficit grew larger, and the White House insisted on unraveling the nation's defenses against radical Islamic terror, more and more Americans began to feel the same.

When I returned home to Chicago, I attended the health care town hall meeting of my own congressional representative, Jan Schakowsky. She had stacked the event in advance with bused-in union members and activists from a group called Health Care for America Now (HCAN), who gathered outside the meeting long before the doors opened and filled the room before many local residents had begun to arrive.

A friend and I had brought a video camera, and taped HCAN organizers instructing their followers to block questions and to drown out opposing views. One of the organizers was HCAN's state director, who also worked for Citizen Action Illinois, a Left-wing group in which Rep.

Schakowsky served in an official advisory capacity. It seemed likely that she knew of and approved of the suppression of her constituents' views. Citizen Action had, in fact, been founded by Rep. Schakowsky's husband, Robert Creamer. He resigned in 1997 after being investigated for check-kiting at Citizen Action's predecessor, Public Action. In 2006, he was convicted and sent to federal prison. There, he wrote a book that called for health care reform in 2009, and sketched a ten-point plan for carrying it out, which Democrats followed to the letter. The plan included creating an artificial sense of crisis about the health care system, demonizing private insurance, and rolling out a nationwide network of "grassroots" organizations to control public opinion.

After watching that plan unfold in my own hometown, I finally made the decision to run for Congress. I felt that our district deserved a representative who listened to the residents instead of lecturing us. It was a long-shot race in a district that hadn't elected a Republican in decades. But I knew that the people of Chicago and Cook County were tired of being abused by the corrupt Democrat machine, now running the country as well as the city. More than that, I knew people wanted a fresh start, a reassurance that we could put old battles aside and return to the common-sense principles that built our city and our nation.

These were principles I had explored at Harvard, where at times I had felt I was expected to "unlearn" such notions. They were also principles I had explored through the test of experience and the heat of debate. And each new experience and debate—with Barney Frank, Jan Schakowsky, and beyond—has affirmed them.

15

THE LEPTOGONIANS

Growing Up Conservative in a Disrupted Decade

James Poulos

The unholy trinity of big-think social commentary—decades analysis, generations analysis, and the analysis of one's own personal story—are as popular as they are perilous. Together, they're as reflexively snarked upon by the commentariat as they are relied upon to show us, time and again, who we are and what we're doing. For a certain sort of person who reached adulthood in the 2000s, it's as uncomfortable to jettison these frameworks as it is to measure one's life by them. Many young conservatives—I am one—who were not to the movement born have nonetheless wound up professionalizing their political disposition, in print, on television, online, and in strange hybrids of these media. Our long, late decade has paralleled and reinforced the unscripted character of their lives, in a way persistently at odds with what appears to be the uniform and official quality of the mechanism that often produces pundits on the right. The way these quasi-itinerants have grown up conservative in a disrupted decade is not just interesting; it is important—to our understanding of conservatism and careerism in America. For these unorthodox members of a rising generation, it has never been enough to be conservative and important. On top of these things—and, at times, beyond them—they have insisted on being *interesting*.

There is no way to get disgustingly rich and famous from being the most interesting conservative you can be. On the evidence of the past ten years, I avow that you can't make a living at it. You cannot even win a prize. This is a shame, because I have slowly learned, after brushes with stardom as a bad boy novelist and a brooding, indie-glam front man, that there's no other way I'd find getting disgustingly rich and famous to be worth it. Talking about wealth and fame in this way is unrefined, but studies show that high school seniors and college freshmen want those things together more than everything else combined. And they are being trained to do whatever it takes. Public opinion, alas, is more unsympathetic to my plight than the kiddies'. They, after all, can no longer count on the investment bank or the Internet startup to spirit them into the Promised Land. I and my fellow travelers, on the other hand, never started counting. We were after something different, and we acted like it.

Once alerted to your conservatism, most people do not believe you when you tell them you are interesting. They chalk up your worldly exploits and subtleties of spirit to an unearned luxury—the product of unresolved internal contradictions, lazy hypocrisy, or subterranean false consciousness. Faced with this kind of misunderstanding and disappointment—few celebrities or organization kids can cope with it unmedicated—the dutiful life of a family man offers a refuge of joy and repose that fame and fortune cannot. This is especially the case when you are married, as am I, to a former television actress and brooding trip hop front woman. Those brushed enough with stardom lose the longing to dip. Even on the DC happy-hour circuit—to the young professional conservative, what the Greyhound bus terminal in Hollywood is to the aspiring actress—the gnarled, attention-grasping sinews relax . . . the mind unfolds from its customary fist shape . . . you no longer find yourself thinking of yourself as the Kanye West of the Right-wing blogosphere.

Given booze enough and time, you discover there are interesting conservatives all around you. Most interesting of all, you very gradually discover that many of them stand in ambiguous, unsettled relation to professional conservatism—though their profession, one way or the other, is, indeed, to be conservative . . . one way or the other.

In a disrupted decade such as the 2000s, the absence of neat and streamlined career paths, even in a city as captive to them as Washington, should surprise no one. But the farm system or pipeline that professionalizes conservatives into "the movement" is so seemingly self-sufficient and self-perpetuating that the deeper story of professional conservatives who are *not* products of the pipeline goes obscured. The consequent judgment that professional conservatives, as a rule, are more wholly and comfortably committed to their outfit and its practices than the average Marine is to his reinforces the prejudice that professional conservatism is a closed system, a place where people with no outside interests or abilities go to congratulate each other, in business casual over bad gin and tonics, for being more conventional, more upstanding, and, of course, more right—in Nixon-speak, *more Orthogonian*—than everyone else. Amid the endless disruptions of the '00s, movement wonkery and punditry attained such a preternatural flatline in their "message discipline" that people who were not conservatives for a living could be excused for mistaking caricature for reality. But even within the industry, the suspicion can no longer be dismissed that some of conservatism's marquee institutions and personalities are too vulnerable to the sort of contemptuous ridicule enjoyed by regular people who are certain that conservatives—*professional* conservatives, above all—must be unfit for life off the reservation, unable and unwilling to function in any truly human environment.

Among those of us who have marked out our irregular twenties during this uneven, unquiet decade are conservatives who cannot in any coherent sense be called Orthogonian. We have not lived our lives at Right angles. Nor have we lived them obtusely, jutting out to the Left. Our angles, though a bit off-center, open acutely to the Right. My fellow blogger at Postmodern Conservative, the young math theorist Will Wilson, instructed me once that a curve "whose kurtosis is slightly smaller than ortho" is what's known as a "leptokurtic" curve. "Presumably," he concluded, "a *leptogonal* angle is slightly narrower than an orthogonal one."

That makes us—Leptogonians.

Conservatives Are People Too! is the name of a book that will probably be written but should never be published. In the best magazine article on the demise of the society-and-politics Web site Culture11—I was its first and last political editor—*Washington Monthly* editor Charles Homans provoked me to say that the conservative movement could use, and should welcome, more repentant and recovering twenty- or thirtysomethings—freshly minted adults whose look back on their dissolute, dysfunctional, and possibly undignified young lives leaves them ready to raise their expectations. I stand by this remark, but Glenn Beck was not who I had in mind. When it comes to Becks who proffer culture commentary, I prefer my hipster hero Beck Hansen, whose conservative soul distills more wisdom into a few bars than the therapeutic pundit—call him a therapundit—can muster in a whole TV harangue: "This town is crazy / and nobody cares / Baby you're lost / baby you're a lost cause."

Glenn Beck must not have been a lost cause, because here he is, recovering addict and ADHD diagnosée, a professional conservative disgustingly rich and famous. It seems the phenomenon termed "the triumph of the therapeutic" by my nerd hero, Philip Rieff, has outfoxed me once again: in a world where therapy is woven into the fabric of human experience, casualties of the soft bigotry of liberal permissiveness are likely to work as conservatives in the same emotional register as the liberally permissive themselves. If Rush Limbaugh is the Right's Oprah Winfrey, as Reihan Salam has suggested, Glenn Beck is surely its Tyra Banks.

Possibly I failed to see how the Glenn Becks of the world figured into my vision because Glenn Beck is not at all from the generational cohort I had in mind—mine. Born in 1964, Beck is two years the junior of another therapundit: Chuck Palahniuk, whose immortal *Fight Club* is nearly as profound an apparent monument to the 2000s as Glenn Beck's *The Christmas Sweater.* Palahniuk opened our long, disrupted decade just as Beck finished it out: by imposing an instantly accessible, fully comprehensive worldview onto our national character, and insisting that we have no real choice but to partake of it. Where psychotherapy supplies the patient with an analytical framework that allows him to cope with the pathologies underlying his symptoms, therapunditry makes patients of us all by analyzing the whole world as an inescapable crisis that can never be cured. Only commitment to a certain attitude or approach, to a way of seeing the world, will suffice as a coping mechanism. We are disentitled to make sense of the world as it is and as we are, and to organize our responses accordingly. Whatever it may be, the political upshot of this therapeutic view is ancillary to the personal:

> *We're the middle children of history, man. No purpose or place. We have no Great War. No Great Depression. Our Great War is a spiritual war. Our Great Depression is our lives.*

As the movie *Fight Club* made famous: "I can't get married," Ed Norton's character complains to Brad Pitt's Tyler Durden. "I'm a thirty-year-old boy." Deep thoughts, for the twenty-year-old boy in the audience nursing a vague but powerful urge to be the next Bret Easton Ellis (or is it David Bowie?). But ten years on, that thirty-year-old husband and father laughs. *You think that's depressing? How about "I can't get married. I'm a forty-year-old virgin."* It's Judd Apatow, three years younger again than Glenn Beck, who better understands that, for those who came of age within them, the '00s weren't about great, epochal depressions but pervasive, low-intensity disruptions. The *Fight Club* fantasy of creating lives of chaos loses its romance in a decade defined by the unreliability of personal, professional, and political structures and by the unpredictability of events. Though it sounded right at the time—who couldn't relate to a guy with an all-consuming desire to face-punch Jared Leto into oblivion?—Durden's credo proved to be a bitter last gasp of nostalgia for a menu of life choices narrowed dramatically by world-historical circumstance.

For millennial spokesmen like Benjamin Kunkel, born 1972, that conditioning isn't a dream but a nightmare. *Indecision*, his debut novel released in 2005 (exactly midway between *Fight Club* and the children's version of *The Christmas Sweater*), viewed 9/11 from the perspective of Dwight Wilmerding, a supposedly characteristic '00s twenty-eight-year-old. Dwight's formative experience is the end of the Cold War, which is analogized to his parents' bad marriage. As, I think, with Beck, coping with parental failure animates the wounded souls of both *Fight Club* and *Indecision*. Where Palahniuk responds with a call to orphans to find their solidarity in violence, Kunkel finds them seeking togetherness in the safe space of a structured environment. For Kunkel, the '90s embodied just that juvenile fantasy—a post-political redemption of all the '80s childhoods ruined by failed marriages, "a permanent future that we can rely on!" Or, because the line is delivered in an ecstasy puddle (during the dawn hours of 9/11), "Warm milk and guaranteed tender safety for all honest mammals willing to work a twenty-hour week!" This is post-politics with the state as genderless parent—one that's, impossibly, as cool as it is loving. *Where the Wild Things Are* meets *Romper Room* meets Nerve.

For Kunkel, the childish ridiculousness of this utopian decade, imaginable up to the minute before the towers were struck, is admittedly self-conscious. But that's a badge of pride. Its poetry, as liberal philosopher Richard Rorty taught our latchkey coeds, must still be taken seriously—as our only possible source of inspiration. May I present Dwight Wilmerding's credo:

> *Everyone sort of being gay! Or lesbian! Free public psychoanalysis for everyone! Lavish state-funded group therapy in the nude! Very colorful umbrellas and no more rain!*

Dwight's is the consummate therapunditry, prescribing our nation of patients nothing more or less than itself. The medium is the message. The self-realized hell on earth of Palahniuk's transcendent homosexual allegory (a queerness lost on me in 1999) is to be replaced, in the minds of anyone who had ever had hope for the '00s, with the self-realized heaven on earth of a transcendently pansexual up-past-bedtime story.

Or so we are led to believe. But—*Conservatives Are People Too!* We Leptogonians had greater hopes for the disrupted decade that dragged us into adulthood! But we have little use for state funding and none for group therapy, and we are as disagreeable about public nudity as we are about twirling umbrellas on a clear blue day.

Though they're almost of the same generation as we Leptogonians, who entered our thirtieth decade as the twenty-first century entered its second, people like Kunkel are put off by our cultural dispositions. Again, the politics is merely symptomatic: the root pathology is that we're dreaming the wrong dreams. Kunkel, a founder of the very colorful *n + 1* umbrella group, may himself be decadent enough a curator of his vibrant social network to count among his friends conservatives who have written novels and played in real live rock bands, painted a picture or built a house. He has probably even exchanged e-mails with a conservative who has read *Indecision*.

When I made to Charles Homans the remarks that I did, I had in mind someone less like Glenn Beck and more like Dwight Wilmerding—though even Dwight is hardly Leptogonian material. Dwight has a *condition*, abulia, a medically treatable inability to *make* decisions; we Leptogonians have a *predicament* we decline to medicate, manifest in our habitual *excess* of decisions. Bands, blogs, books, PhDs, businesses, babies, new lives in new places: over time, at least, these are not either/or propositions. Dwight's catharsis is the possibility of release from life as a chronic patient; we Leptogonians struggle not over agency itself but over *which* kind of agent to be, and when, and for how long. Our chronic failure to accept Plato's dictum, *one man, one art*, has led us on a sometime goose chase, sometime minotaur hunt more in accordance with the oracular Socratic credo *know thyself.* Marx was writing bad poetry when he dreamed of hunting at dawn, fishing at noon, cattle-rustling at sunset, and writing essays like this one "after dinner, just as I have a mind, without ever becoming hunter, fisherman, shepherd, or critic." But we have been—and still are and will be—musicians, screenwriters, scholars, artists, or craftsmen, builders and makers of larger or smaller but invariably human-proportioned things. Cosmopolitan boys and girls not quite as high in the culture club as Benjamin Kunkel may not know how to believe it, but it is the truth, written across the years of our Leptogonian lives.

My case is exemplary but unexceptional. Like Mark Hemingway, *Washington Examiner* columnist and editor, I was in a band before I blogged a word about politics. When Mark meets new people, and riffs on playing the 9:30 Club or sharing a stage with Stellastarr,* "it's always assumed I'm one of *them*. When they later find out the same guy goes to the Lutheran church every week and worked at *National Review*, it just does not compute." (He calls this "the riddle of Mark Hemingway.") I put together my band after an upstairs neighbor came down to ask about the noise and handed me her *Rolling Stone* business card. We had a manager and an attorney before we had a demo, and we filmed a video in Glen Ballard's High Window studio the day Marlon Brando died in a hospital across town. Nobody asked about my politics. Then again, I didn't tell. The only exception: my drummer, press man for Consumer Watchdog and longtime volunteer for TreePeople. He was my closest friend in LA. We're still recording music.

Like Sam Goldman, I left the sweat and the stage for academia. One recent evening I found Sam donning suit and tie to catch a Lincoln Center performance of Webern's piano music—fat, dark bruise still pulsing from the head punch he had taken the night before in the mosh pit at the Cro-Mags show. At my behest, he reflected on his long friendship, forged onstage and off in the hard-core scene, with crack Lefty pundit Spencer Ackerman. Out of reflex, you might suspect Sam Goldman to be a blogger at Think Progress, or the brainchild of the Vote or Die campaign; but Sam blogs at Pomocon, and he is the brainchild of a dissertation on Spinoza's theologico-political theory. No, he doesn't shave his head anymore—nor do I wear eyeliner. But he still considers "the way participants in hard-core create and preserve relations of trust and responsibility—without a party platform or formal institutions" to be a good example "of the kind of organic, noninstrumental association conservatives should respect." I can add another. LA's vampirism and gangrene of soul were always poised to corrupt me forever, but that was half the charm of LA as I sought out the girl for me. When she found me, by the grace of God, the spell was broken. A month after we met, my wife-to-be broke up her band, I broke up mine, and soon after that we were gone.

Like J. P. Freire, who came to the *Examiner* by way of *The American Spectator*, I came to DC because I knew that was where the movement was. "There's no way I would have considered going into journalism," J. P. told me not long ago, had there not been a job "greeting me right out of college." He would have "gone into management consulting, or taken a job at some Fortune 500 company that was in my hometown or somewhere in New York. I just would've started doing the recruiting thing," he said. "I would've met with job recruiters and tried to see where I'd wind up." Professional conservatism offers a philosophy and aesthetic independent of the American career pipeline, which we Leptogonians characteristically reject. For all the blows *Fight Club* landed in its assault on the anonymity and ennui of corporate life, Tyler Durden had to send an army of anti-interns to blow up the home offices of the credit card companies. Back then, the system still stood on its own two feet. We Leptogonians have since watched corporate America knock *itself* down and blow itself up. Handing your future over to the firm was a hard enough sell before the bailouts. Today we're the ones bailing out.

Naturally enough, we Leptogonians are more concerned than others when we see the movement take on key features of just another industrial complex. In the inevitable way, of course, everything does—we nurse no romantic ideal here, place no faith in professional communitarianism, distributivism, or anarcho-syndicalism. We shudder at the phrase *human resources*. Instead, we share a guiding understanding that the institutional pathologies that eat away at the integrity of one's life can be kept at bay if the popular, default vision of a career is dispensed with. This is not without its risks and costs, psychological and financial. But it is the soul of American individualism, and it is quietly coming back.

The cultural ethos shared by us Leptogonians is a badly needed counterweight to the therapunditocratic credo. The ordeal of the '00s has shown Leptogonians that we really are competent to chart—and rechart—our own courses, without subserving our souls to a master narrative prescribed to help us cope with a degree of disruption out of all proportion to human resourcefulness and individual responsibility. Leptogonians who are professional conservatives tend to come at their line of work in the recognition that they are wanderers at heart. It's right there in the grammar: not even seminomads can truly be at home in a movement, no matter how conservative.

It would be wrong, however, to think of Leptogonians as the conservative version of homeless people. The maturity needed to govern one's peregrinations—a maturity that, at bottom, must be learned—points the wanderer toward the sorts of homes one can carry on one's back. Last year, Michael Brendan Dougherty, contributing editor to *The American Conservative* and 2009 Phillips Journalism Fellow, left DC to move close to home, get married, and "start writing fiction again." Before he came to DC, a certain "dyspeptic conservative thinker from Rockford, Illinois" had warned him "not to stay more than three years at a time"—good advice, he told me. The allure of professional conservatism, he said, "can begin with one unshakeable intellectual conviction in college, like 'Entrepreneurs are awesome' or 'modernity is chaos'—and suddenly you are part of a movement staffed with other bright, young, idealistic conservatives who think, drink, and talk like you. But the movement's institutions invite young, talented, idealistic conservatives to do one of two things"—sell out for the movement or against it, defending "whatever the Republican Party does" or "badmouthing fellow conservatives." Walk the line, and "you're likely to be accused of disloyalty by the hacks" and "hackery by the principled and aloof." Faced with the choice between "a secure gig in the movement's intellectual ghetto" and "a higher-status, but more insecure, job at a respected outlet," Michael chose neither. "Around the holidays," he told me, "my family likes to remind me that I'm some Right-winger. Maybe, but I don't belong to the movement anymore."

That DC is often a place where careers find you, rather than the inverse, is a bug *and* a feature. Elizabeth Nolan Brown, another twenty-seven-year-old writer who moved recently to New York, put it plainly. "When I was in DC, I forgot that I had other interests besides politics, journalism, blogging, et cetera." Once "heavily involved" in theater, dance, and fiction, she "totally stopped" for her three years in Washington. In the hands of us Leptogonians, that kind of focus is a constructive ambiguity—in the way politics would be if representatives, by choice and not by law, term-limited themselves. Like movement conservatism, professional conservatism requires an ebb and flow of gifted amateurs. But what may benefit the Right most of all is what Americans, in politics and beyond, are longing to experience again: an end to hackocracy, with its heinous fusion of celebrity cult and corporate careerism that cuts across lines of party and sector and industry and class. If the Right is to prosper from this groundswell over the next ten years, much will be owed to Leptogonian effort. The hacks and the therapundits have seized the nation's attention, but they cannot hold its *interest*.

16

THE SMOKER'S CODE

Helen Rittelmeyer

In 2008, the year I graduated from Yale, April 20 fell on a Sunday. That was a problem for the Party of the Right. We had intended to hold our protest against the drug war on April 20, the traditional day, but cross-scheduling our rally with Sunday church services would have cut our turnout in half. (If you don't know the significance of the number 4/20 to the war on drugs, ask one in five American teenagers.) After some debate, the libertarians caved to the traditionalists and rescheduled Yale Conservatives Against the Drug War—aka "Tweed for Weed"—for the following Saturday.

Moving the date of the protest paid off. Even the more Right-wing Christians who weren't exactly *for* weed showed up with signs that said THE DRUG WAR BREAKS UP FAMILIES. The rest of the Christians got the signs the libertarians had made for them: I COULDN'T PROTEST THE DRUG WAR ON 4/20 BECAUSE I WAS IN CHURCH.

It's amazing in retrospect that the Party of the Right could be so ecumenical, given that we were split almost evenly between two ideological factions that should have been at each other's throats. At one extreme were the anarcho-capitalists, whose ringleader was a Dumpster-diving mountain man from Idaho who spent his gap year teaching English in a Chinese whorehouse. (Fluent girls get better rates.) I shared an apartment with a couple of them the summer after graduation, and I can't remember them ever toasting anything but "Smash the state!" That same summer bred an interfactional romance not involving me, which led to the following exchange between my female housemate and her Glee Club director:

"The chip in my passport doesn't work. Will that be a problem when we go to South America?"

"I'm not sure. What happened to it?"

"My anarchist ex-boyfriend microwaved it to free me from the state."

Opposite the libertarians was a merry band of pre–Vatican II Catholics whose record at winning converts for Mother Church was so consistent that the POR soon got a not-entirely-flattering reputation for being a "Catholic factory." I was one of these, and a religious studies major on top of that, although I can't say I ever captured any heathen scalps myself. I watched most of the theological drama from the sidelines, occasionally laying bets on which souls would flip. On one particularly good Easter, I won two bottles of gin, but I felt so crass for gambling bottles of liquor on my friends' salvation that I immediately invited over my newly minted coreligionists and the two losing bettors to split the winnings. At least once a month, someone from the Catholic faction would drink too much on Saturday night and oversleep the last mass of the day at five p.m.

When I wonder how we managed to have such party solidarity despite everyone's ideological differences, I suppose that it was partly because our libertarians tended to be Southerners and Westerners who cared as much about manliness and personal honor as our traditionalists, and partly because our Catholics were more dissipated than our anarchists. I'm sure that the foxhole mentality of being conservatives on an Ivy League campus helped. But I think the glue that really held us together was the fact that, conservative or libertarian, we all smoked like busted tailpipes.

Fusionism was the theory. When I let two libertarians use the cover page of my Bible to roll some fine loose Turkish tobacco when they'd run out of papers, that was the practice.

It wasn't just that nothing breeds mutual affection like huddling under a shop overhang in a New Haven sleet storm because Anna Liffey's won't let you smoke inside anymore. We smoked on principle. It was reactionary, libertarian, spiritual, and aesthetic all at the same time. *Cigarettes Are Sublime*, Richard Klein's tribute to nicotine, was our Bible, because it had sentences like this: "When the religious dignity of smoking is completely obscured, we have lost a right to pray in public."

That our tobacco habit had something to do with freedom should be obvious. We were lucky enough to have one bar nearby that still allowed smoking inside—the Owl Shop, a cigar bar—but the cheaper places hounded us out into the New Haven cold, in accordance with Connecticut law. During my four years at Yale, it seemed like every other week brought news of another city banning smoking in bars, which we took as proof of an incipient police state.

But it was never simply a matter of personal liberty, which, after all, wasn't something the traditionalists always cared about. Most of us were in favor of banning prostitution, for instance, in spite of the libertarian mountain man's assurances that all the prostitutes he'd met in China were the salt of the earth. Smoking bans bothered us because they gave the modern cult of health the force of law, which was more than we thought it deserved. The little joys of cigarette smoking—a moment of late-night camaraderie, an excuse to talk to an attractive stranger, just the right prop for an emphatic gesture, or simply a moment of relaxation at the end of a long day—these were all more important to us than health. There was something unappealingly technocratic about the state's attempt to boil the argument down to heart-disease rates. Unlike the libertarians, we thought smokers *should* have to make a convincing case that the benefits of smoking in bars outweigh the costs. Unlike the Left, we thought unquantifiables like the way good bourbon mixes with a Marlboro should count.

The other hot front in the war on tobacco in those days was the campaign to airbrush cigarettes out of classic movies, which sounds ridiculous the first time you hear about it but struck a chord with the Party of the Right. Cary Grant and Lauren Bacall—or Lou Reed and Nico, depending—had a lot to do with how and why we smoked. None of us was ashamed to admit it, either. When the skeptics tritely accused us of only smoking in order to seem cool, we took it to mean that cigarettes have an aesthetic beauty even puritans can't deny. Arguments from aesthetics came in handy in political debates, too. The party once debated the topic *Resolved: Patriotism is glorified brand loyalty*, and the prevailing opinion on the floor was that yes, it is, and no, we don't care, because brand loyalty can be a powerful moral force. Consuming a particular product means living up to its image—a Parliament tastes like a Lucky Strike, but it matters which one a person chooses to smoke. Back in his college days at Oxford, Oscar Wilde complained, "I find it harder and harder every day to live up to my blue china," and he was only half-kidding. Men start acting more gentlemanly when they put on nice suits, which is why POR debates had a strict dress code. In the same way, the responsibility of behaving like an American makes people a little more self-reliant and freedom-loving than they would otherwise be, just as being British stiffens the upper lip when foreigners are watching. Brand loyalty and patriotism are all parts of a person's reputation, which is just another word for something demanding to live up to.

The way we figured it, lighting a cigarette imposes the same kind of expectations, which after four years of talking about it grew into something we referred to as the smoker's code. First rule: you are duty-bound to give a light to anyone who asks for it, no matter how humble. As someone once said, if Prometheus had stolen fire from heaven to light his cigarette, the gods would have let him do it. Second rule: there is no such thing as owing someone a cigarette, because keeping count of how many smokes someone has bummed from you is petty and gauche. The third rule, which covered everything else: no cowardly, classless, un-seductive, or painfully earnest behavior unbecoming a smoker. You're smoking a cigarette, so act like it.

Our devotion to style as something of deep moral importance made sense, given the strange kind of traditionalists we were. Fifties nostalgists and canon chauvinists were our allies, certainly, but no trad in the POR was boring enough to agree with them. My own special nemesis was what we called the "fence" idea of traditionalism, after Chesterton's thought experiment about the man who sees an apparently useless fence across a road. Don't tear something down because you can't see the use in it, Chesterton said. "Go away and think. Then, when you can come back and tell me that you *do* see the use of it, I may allow you to destroy it."

I hated that fence. For one thing, there are plenty of instances where it's impossible to know why a particular tradition was created, and, in those cases, fence traditionalism means nothing more than having a higher threshold for how bad things have to get before you're willing to change—weak sauce, not the stuff counterrevolutions are made of. But mostly I hated the fence because it paints an uninspiring picture of tradition as a concession to human ignorance. Humans *are* ignorant—"the individual is foolish, but the species is wise," said Burke—but my own traditionalism felt less like resignation and more like falling in love. When I decided to start taking Catholicism seriously, it wasn't because the Church offered arguments that convinced me of anything, or because I thought she was so old she must be right. It was because, when confronted by the totality of a beautiful institution, I fell hard. Becoming a smoker was the same. I wanted what the smokers had, and, if the only way to get it was to let them lead me into behaviors I didn't quite understand, so be it.

Traditions and rituals put flesh on the bare bones of an idea, giving it a personality. When you make an idea more like a person, you transform it from something you believe into something you can love. You can't fall in love with a fence, except in Massachusetts.

The anarcho-capitalists didn't care one way or the other about tradition, but they did care about honor, which, next to style, was the theme of the smoker's code that mattered most to the Party of the Right. For reasons we never quite articulated, smoking felt like a rebellion against Yale's moral consensus that the two most important things in life are for everyone to be happy and for everyone to get along. It may have had something to do with our favorite cigarette-smoking archetypes—reporters, aristocrats, and thieves—all of whom fit the description I once read someone give of turn-of-the-century yellow journalists: "I don't think they had an ounce of morality between them, but they had a very acute sense of honor." Or, to pick a line from Raymond Chandler's description of the perfect noir hero, "I think he might seduce a duchess, and I am quite sure he would not spoil a virgin." Our libertarians may have written off opposition to drugs and prostitution as uptight Catholic moralizing, but they would have eaten their own teeth before betraying a fellow party member, even one they hated.

The party needed a culture of honor, given how much of our time was spent fighting with each other. We were brawlers who didn't think it was a good night unless someone got eviscerated on the debate floor. The advantage of honor over boring old ethics is that it sees violence not as the regrettable outcome of a breakdown in your moral system, but as an important and admirable expression of it, provided the fight is conducted by the proper rules. (No eye-gouging.) Other kinds of morality try to minimize violence, even the metaphorical kind, on the logic that cooperation and persuasion yield better outcomes. This hardly gives conflict its due. I always preferred the motto of one of my personal heroes in the POR: "I only believe in violence when it's absolutely unnecessary."

Our constant philosophical brawling had its costs—one party member who had been raised the son of evangelical missionaries got his belief in God knocked out of him the same semester he was serving as president of a Yale Bible study group. (He served out his term, of course. It was an honor thing.) One girl joined the POR as a Left-wing, Riot-Grrrl lesbian and left it a Right-wing, Catholic, celibate lesbian. The constant throwing of philosophical punches produced plenty of casualties like these, if you want to call them that. It also made us brothers-in-arms whose loyalty to each other was unshakable. The old saying that sums up the way we felt: "Nobody hits my little brother but me."

It might not be apparent from my description that the POR's strange brand of conservatism has anything to offer the modern movement, so let me close with the story of a time when our very undergraduate ethos had a head-on collision with the grown-up world, which is also the story of the time I thoroughly humiliated myself in front of Ross Douthat. A few months after I graduated, the Intercollegiate Studies Institute invited Douthat to Yale to speak at their conference on "The Future of Conservatism," and, since I was living in New York at the time, I popped up to New Haven for the weekend. During the Q&A, I asked Douthat why he always addressed his blog to the Left rather than to his fellow conservatives, and what he hoped to accomplish by embracing the dubious mantle of "respectable" conservatism. I think I even used the word "token," which, given his move from the *Atlantic* to the *New York Times* four months later, was prescient.

"Well," he explained, "take the article I just published in the *Atlantic*—'Is Pornography Adultery?' I wasn't trying to get the *Atlantic*'s audience on board with the whole of the Catholic Church's teachings on sex and marriage. I just want them to consider the possibility that maybe, in certain circumstances, pornography shouldn't be totally and unreservedly celebrated. I'm going one baby-step at a time."

The Q&A started to wrap up, and I remembered that there was still free coffee in the foyer, so I got up from my seat while Douthat was answering his final question. Just as I reached the door, he referred back to my question.

"As I said to the blond girl in the front row . . . hey, wait! Where are you going?" I froze.

Now, what I should have done was politely resume my seat and let the man continue with his answer. What I actually did was widen my eyes, look to the left and to the right ("What, you mean *me*?"), and then, with great, exaggerated tiptoe steps, walk backward out of the room.

The last thing I heard before I shut the door behind me was Douthat saying, "Hey, come back!" and the audience laughing.

As soon as I heard the murmur of chatter through the door, I knew it was safe to come back in. A distant acquaintance of mine, named Peter, walked up to me and said, "That was a perfect metaphor." I told him I did not think my red-faced embarrassment was a metaphor for anything.

"No, it's a metaphor for why Douthat is wrong. We don't need little baby-steps. We need grand, unapologetic theatricality."

I still felt mortified—Mr. Douthat, if you're reading this, I'm very sorry—but Peter was right that the party's bombastic style and Douthat's meliorism make a good compare-and-contrast. Douthat believes in putting forward good arguments that the other side will understand. The POR believes that the best way to convince someone you're right is to make what you're doing look good. We preferred embodying conservative values to articulating them, according to St. Francis's advice: "Preach the gospel without ceasing; if necessary, use words." P. J. O'Rourke is a good Franciscan; he makes the Left worry that, by rejecting conservatism, they're missing out on a good time. The best way to convince someone you're right is to make what you're doing look good, and a cigarette properly held goes a long way in that direction.

17

FREE TO SERVE

Bill Rivers,
University of Delaware 2010

The campfire's sharp-scented wood smoke rises in a silvery cloud into a night sky pinpricked by starlight and washed by a pale half of an early spring moon. "God's fingernail," someone jokes below, one of forty students gathered about the fire in the basin of a bowl in the Kentucky mountains.

"Nurse Steve," a homegrown Delawarean and a senior Nursing major at the university, has found a tattered straw hat to accompany his paint-stained overalls. He beams with pride under its brim, and I begin to feel much better about my purple gardening gloves—the only ones I could find as I rushed to pack for the trip.

Of the forty others, I know only a handful: Lauren is a junior from inner-city Baltimore. She tells me she had difficulty getting to sleep when she first came to college—the absence of wailing sirens throughout the night kept her awake—and I wonder what she thinks of the still mountain dark.

Seated on the log bench, beside her is my friend Karyn. A floormate of mine, Karyn invited me to go on the mission trip twenty-four hours prior to its departure from the university. A freshman, like me, she is new to this, and neither of us is sure what to expect.

This group of forty traveled six hundred miles from Newark, Delaware, to Harlan County, Kentucky, in a five-van caravan of rambling ten-seaters and jam-packed Suburbans, striking out first west and then south, winding its way through the blue-misted Appalachians under thick gray clouds. We are all students—in some way or another—from the University of Delaware, on a mission trip sponsored by Intervarsity Christian Fellowship. Some are veterans who bring their own drills and jigsaws, and some, like Karyn and I, are brand-new to it, with nothing but a few tools and my grandmother's purple gardening gloves. When we ask the old-timers what to expect, they shrug and say that every trip is different but that we should have packed a lot of socks. I have three pairs for a week. Strike two.

Though predominantly Christian, our group is diverse, comprising agnostics and atheists, Baptists, Lutherans, Methodists, Presbyterians, Episcopalians, and one purple-gloved Catholic. Among us, we represent ten different states, from California to Maine, and almost every department at the University of Delaware. Some of us can quote their favorite Bible passages by heart while others know that the Bible is a book with other, smaller books in it. Some of the group can trace their ancestry back to *The Mayflower*; others are first-generation Americans, English by no means their first language.

We are encouraged to get to bed early on this, the first night of spring break 2007. We will rise early, "suit up" (as Nurse Steve says, thumbs tucked proudly in the corners of his overalls), eat, gather our tools, and be at our work sites by eight a.m. the following morning. After washing the last of the Kraft macaroni and cheese dinner from our plastic bowls, we gather about the fire's dying embers for a brief Bible reading and a soft prayer for good work the coming week. Cell phone reception being nonexistent in our little canyon, we lie in the dusty bunks of the camp cabins and share jokes—the late Mitch Hedberg is a favorite—and drop, one by one, to sleep.

Our work site lies nestled deep in the blue hills of Appalachia. In mid-March, the buds on the trees are just beginning to open; tiny splashes of vibrant pink and bright violet on cool, gray bark. Columns of mist rise from the valleys in the wake of a strong spring rain that came sometime in the night. Between these ridges, our work crew's van follows a strip of asphalt called Route 1274, which winds its way up and down and around the mountains. The road is an artery of commerce feeding a thin tissue of local businesses and residential areas (shanty houses and worn-out homes) that cluster closely alongside. Nearly a third of the county's ten thousand families live below the poverty line.

This land, one of the few designated impoverished areas of the United States, is *poor*. Lyndon Johnson had places like Harlan County in mind when he planned his war on poverty over forty years ago. From the looks of things, the end to that war is nowhere in sight.

Karyn and I are in the same crew for the week and our job detail appears to be light work: put in some new windows and paint the house. I'm almost disappointed. Nurse Steve's group is assigned to *build* a house. Our project is a leaning one-story structure, set not more than twenty feet back from an offshoot of the main highway. It is early morning when we first meet the owner of the place, and it is around that time that I begin to feel the change.

Miss Loretta has a face that has seen much of the hard side of life. Her forehead and cheekbones are etched with many lines, and her pointy, defiant nose and jaw seem worn down by the passage of time. Yet hers is a strong face, with stern, piercing eyes, and I know I have met only a few people in my life as tough and vital as this thin, old woman from the back hills of Kentucky. Loretta lives with her older sister—a tiny bundle of a human being, bedridden inside in the dark of the old house, wrapped tightly in blankets. Loretta's sister (we never learned her name) has lost her sight recently due to illness and cannot walk by herself. She is totally dependent upon Miss Loretta.

Our first meeting is awkward. We are an alien sight, strangers almost to each other, in eclectic outfits of old clothes, work boots, and overalls, standing before a proud woman three times our age. Miss Loretta does not say much, other than to thank us for the work we will do. She relaxes visibly when she sees the carpenter assigned to lead our work crew, a local Harlan County man named Johnny.

Johnny is part of the Christian Outreach for the Appalachian People (COAP), the organization that invited us down for the week, and the point of contact between the students and the families we're here to serve. A native Kentuckian and a resident of Harlan County, Johnny is someone Loretta knows. It is up to him to be the bridge between Loretta and her sister, and the gangly crew of students on their front porch.

"Those some mighty pretty gloves you got there," he says, looking at me. Abracadabra.

Tall with sun-browned skin and a short, dark beard, Johnny is soft-spoken with a fantastically dry sense of humor. His gibes about my purple gardening gloves are delivered in a thick Kentuckian accent, and soon our group is comfortable and relaxed. The best thing about Kentucky, he tells us, is the road leading into it from Tennessee.

"Gonna fix your house up, Loretta," Johnny tells the old woman. She thanks him, and says their last winter was a cold one. The drafty windows no longer keep the little house warm. Overhearing this, and with the image of Miss Loretta's disabled, bundled sister freshly in mind, we become aware of the purpose to our work. With renewed vigor and under Johnny's direction, we break into teams to scrape off the old, flaking coat of paint as Loretta returns inside to take care of her sister.

As we prep for painting, Johnny sets about taking measurements for the new windows, his calloused fingers making quick, precise marks on the siding with a battered pencil. We talk while we work, and slowly, cautiously, our group gets to know itself. Rebecca is a senior, preparing to graduate and go into the "real world." She's anxious about finding work. Karyn and I are freshmen, with only one full semester behind us. Justin, a sophomore, plays the yo-yo professionally. After much pleading, he agrees to treat us to a world-class performance over lunch.

Becoming more comfortable with each other, we take on other subjects, gingerly at first, then more and more freely: family, politics, and faith. What began as a medley of philosophy and theology then moves into the more serious business of movies and music. Yes, the gangsters in *The Godfather* are supposed to be Catholic. Natasha Bedingfield's music video for "Unwritten" *was* kind of weird, but she won her Grammy Award for the song, not the video.

Lunch comes and we break to eat, with one freshly painted wall of the house shining brightly in the afternoon sun. The four windows have been prepped for evac, the new ones leaning up against Johnny's mud-splattered truck. Justin's yo-yo performance is well received, and afterward we trade stories. I tell the one about the time Granddad blew up his birdfeeder with dynamite while trying to scare off crows. It's a big hit.

Johnny talks too, answering our questions about his family and life in Harlan County. We are surprised to learn that he is in his early forties, and married with four children. He looks much younger. His brother, "the last man to let you down," works at the local cemetery. We can't tell if he's joking. Full of adages and witticisms, Johnny also tells us that it takes two to lie: one to speak it, another to listen.

Regarding Harlan County, Johnny says there is serious trouble with alcohol, a problem that seems endemic to a region where coal mines are giving out and work scarce. But alcoholism and drug abuse are only symptoms of the real problem, which is lack of work. And in the meantime, people's most basic needs—like housing—aren't being met.

This is why COAP got started, and Johnny has worked with them for sixteen years. The organization's local carpenters and builders not only coordinate college groups like ours in the spring, summer, and fall, but also negotiate delivery and donation of housing materials from local construction companies and lumberyards. There is a whole network of men and women in this region, working across different sectors and industries to meet the needs of the community, and COAP appears to be the central nervous system of the whole operation.

After lunch, Johnny focuses on getting the day's work done, but he quietly ensures that we students are the ones to do it. Karyn makes the final measurements for the new window. Justin and I handle the electric saw that makes the final cut. For the next six days, our crew repaints the whole of Miss Loretta's house and installs four new windows. The worst of it comes when we need to replace a part of the wall, but this proves to be the work of a single afternoon. At week's end, there is no denying that we are friends. My purple gloves have become our group's unofficial mascot. In the evenings, we share our stories with the others from Delaware back at our campsite, and we see that they too have come together. Nurse Steve, in his overalls and wide-brimmed hat, has even been given a new nickname: "Tater Farmer."

This community in Harlan County, though impoverished and isolated, possessed the power and the ability to rebuild itself, as Miss Loretta's devotion to her family and COAP's commitment to the two of them clearly demonstrated. While we forty college students came in to do the heavy lifting, the real, true power to alleviate these conditions came from the people who lived there, people moved to such action by their faith.

Coordinating with local businesses, charities, and churches, men and women like Johnny organized work details, arranged lodging for student workers, and secured the resources and materials for the construction projects. We college students simply implemented their vision. Looking at COAP and the experience of Harlan County through an organizational model, we see an effective process of highly democratic mass collaboration, *and it arose naturally from within*. No politician or officeholder in Kentucky's state government or in Washington, DC, led the effort, and no legislation mandated its creation.

COAP was at once both intimate and open. Miss Loretta didn't know us from Adam, but she knew Johnny, a member of her own community, and it was through him that she came to know us. Instead of an outside force of strangers sweeping in for a week to fix her home, Loretta's *neighbors* met her needs, acting in concert with students and volunteers from the outside. Through the men and women of COAP, the concept of mass collaboration, which currently has much of the economic and commercial world abuzz, has been in full effect in rural Appalachia for the past two decades in service of the needy.

COAP also achieved a natural diversity of participants—students and volunteers of varying interests and backgrounds, young and old, Christian (Protestant and Catholic) and nonreligious, from Kentucky, Delaware, and across the country—all without quotas, regulations, or central planning. In striking contrast to government-sponsored programs, COAP efficiently managed and allocated resources. (At the end of the week, our crew had installed four new windows and put two coats of paint on Loretta's house, at which point we packed up and drove to Nurse Steve's site to help his crew finish their house.) It is difficult to imagine any government program achieving the same results as quickly and efficiently, or with as diverse a group of participants, as COAP did.

For some, it is incredibly hard to believe that ordinary, average Americans, if empowered and unencumbered by excessive regulations or financial disincentives, can coalesce and make meaningful changes to better serve the needs of their communities. It seems that only "official," as in government-sponsored and government-driven, initiatives can bring about long-term changes. This mentality is not only misguided, as COAP and the case of Harlan County can attest, but also at odds with over two centuries of our national experience.

Imagine where the world's wealthiest, safest, and freest society would be if, in 1776, its Founders had waited for the ruling government—then the British Empire—to effect change on behalf of the colonists. Was it the federal government that started the civil rights movement in the 1950s? Or was it the efforts of countless nongovernmental actors, some of whom were great leaders like Dr. King, but a vast majority of which were regular Americans from across the country, agitating and laboring courageously through their own organizations? Yet for all that we are told to forge new paths and make our own way (which necessarily includes the ability to *choose to work with others*), the very recent attitude that only government can improve people's lives persists.

There seems to be a distrust of the average, ordinary person to have any stake in doing good works. The idea goes that in the nonpublic realm, if people can't make money off of a venture then no one is going to do it. And since we can't leave people's lives and futures to the whims of the profit motive, government must be the foundation upon which any such activities must take place.

In answer to this charge, the importance of religious faith and its inherent message of service cannot be stated enough. Just as it was in the American Revolution and the civil rights movement, faith was instrumental in bringing change to the people living in the mountains of Kentucky. Faith was the motivation for starting COAP, an organization that opened itself to people of all faiths and backgrounds. Faith created a venue for the kind of mass collaboration that brings real, true change. The same was true of Dr. King's Southern Christian Leadership Conference in the 1960s. Faith then, and now, is a force multiplier that no government program can hope to rival.

Consider the University of Delaware students who journeyed to Kentucky over spring break 2007—hardly a uniform crowd. There were many different motivations for the individuals who went on the trip. Some were simply looking for a change of scenery, some wanted to try something new. Some did indeed have religious reasons behind their desire to serve, but in the end, all were looking to make contact with each other and others. The current generation, constantly capable of getting in touch, longs fiercely to be in touch and COAP, as an organization of people living out their faith, allowed them to do just that.

Through COAP, these forty incredibly diverse college students came to know the paradox of greatness through humble service. In the process, they told their own stories, shared their own hopes and dreams, debating all manner of issues—everything from music to faith—and in so doing, forged new friendships with each other and people living six hundred miles away, whom they might otherwise never have met. The faith-born willingness to serve then is one of society's most precious resources and it can truly work wonders—if we let it.

The mentality that only government can achieve lasting good works removes the opportunity for these kinds of connections and relationships to come to pass. People lose the chance to find themselves and others through service of one another. On top of this, government seldom performs with the efficiency and adaptability of community-inspired programs. In the end, government is simply no replacement for strong, vibrant communities composed of families and willing friends. This is not to say that government plays no role in processes such as these, but its focus should be on unleashing the inherent power of communities.

By laboring to meet Miss Loretta's corporeal needs, we students from the University of Delaware were given an opportunity to nurture our spiritual needs. It is now our responsibility not only to continue to help people like Miss Loretta and her sister wherever we may find them, but also to ensure that others have the chance to do so as well, *for their own sakes* as much as for those of the people they may come to serve. In the end, it is our responsibility to ensure that people remain free to serve.

18

CONSERVATISM FOR PUNKS

Todd Seavey

"This is the issue of this election [1964]: Whether we believe in our capacity for self-government or whether we abandon the American Revolution and confess that a little intellectual elite in a far-distant capital can plan our lives for us better than we can plan them ourselves." —*Ronald Reagan*

"Maybe I'm a prehistoric monster by being an individual. It's highly likely. All I offer to others is their own individuality. Grab it!"

—*Johnny "Rotten" Lydon of the Sex Pistols*

"That myth [that punks are Leftists] got knocked down for me when I learned that Johnny Ramone was a hard-core Republican."

—*Eddie Vedder of Pearl Jam*

I.

It's all happened so quickly, really. In 1964, Barry Goldwater lost the presidential election but won the heart of the Republican Party, turning it decisively in the ostensibly market-oriented yet traditionalist direction we know and love, leading to Reagan, Gingrich, and the familiar think-tanks. Yet 1964 also saw the initial collaboration between Lou Reed and John Cale that would lead to the formation of the Velvet Underground, arguably the first alternative rock band and thus the precursor to punk—to take just one relatively arbitrary example of an American counterculture movement.

One of these two forces, conservatism, is routinely vilified by the media and by youth (conservative campaigners may take short-term solace in the thought that the young don't vote in large numbers, but the young will one day be old, and their youthful allegiances, such as enthusiasm for Obama, will not be entirely forgotten). The other force, punk, is a media darling, respected by highbrow critics and multiple generations of young fans alike. That's not surprising, given its viscerally appealing attitude of rebellion, flashiness, and anarchy.

One of the stupidest recurring mistakes conservatives can make—in a world where the media inevitably shape discourse, in a country founded on freedom and rebellion, and in a world where the cultural battle for the future takes place in the mind of youth—is to accept the mantle of the fuddy-duddies and let the country's free spirits, creative types, young people, and individualists go running to the other camp, where they'll end up, in a tragic non sequitur, aiding and abetting stifling collectivist bureaucracies like the Environmental Protection Agency and money-wasting institutions like the Department of Transportation, not participating in some imagined eternal rock concert of joy and liberation.

In suggesting that the Right try sounding more free-spirited and anarchic, though, am I just advising conservatives to graft foreign components onto their philosophy to win new support, like a triangulating politician who decides, after checking opinion surveys from his district, to be conservative *except on agriculture subsidies*? Not at all. Take my own childhood as an example of how the conservative and punk sensibilities naturally complement each other.

II.

Before an adult life as a New York City media guy, I grew up nerdy and suburban in New England in the final years of the Cold War. I was no ingrate—I recognized, as most Americans do, that we have things pretty good here, and I admired President Reagan for having said so unapologetically and for chastising the Soviets for their failure to learn from our example. And the problem with the Soviets, lest we forget, was not that they lacked religion (subsequent foes have been a reminder that religious people can still be totalitarians) or merely that they had missiles aimed at us (that was a symptom of the conflict, not the source). The problem was that they ruthlessly stifled individual freedom and capitalism.

Our domestic intellectuals—Left or Right—could sneer at pop culture and consumer culture all they liked, but even as a teen I knew enough about history and the state of the rest of the world to know that New Wave albums and local shopping malls were things to be treasured. When Reagan talked about defending America, these things were precisely what I wanted to see defended. They were not just decadent exceptions to a more truly-American social fabric made up solely of farms and churches.

One of the nice things about youthful naïveté (unconservative though any praise of ignorant youth risks being) is that because of not knowing which components of the culture are "supposed" to fit together politically, you might just happen upon a combination that makes more sense than the usual party line.

Take, for example, the assumption that punks are outcasts, lowlifes of a sort. This was hardly my impression back in high school, when the slickest things on TV were punk-influenced videos, and the artiest kids in school—the ones dominating the literary journal and the theater club—were a pantheon of New Wave girls who seemed like an elite, not a gang: from Mary-Alice, the artist with intense red hair buzz cut on the sides and big and wavy on top, to Emma, the short and pale but adorable Australian (an immigrant!) who dressed like a Victorian and had dyed-white hair—not to mention Lisa, the half-Asian Goth chick. They weren't subverting our school so much as running it, and I don't think the Soviets would have liked them one bit. Well, screw the Soviets—and anybody who thinks it's Leftist control freaks like them that make people like our little New Wave elite possible.

Now, some might complain that by embracing New Wave, which was punk made palatable, danceable, and sellable for safe suburban teens, I am simply contributing to bourgeois society's tendency to absorb and water down radical subcultures. Good! What greater testament could there be to the value of bourgeois culture than that it has the capacity to learn from and incorporate the best aspects of radical subcultures without losing its fundamental stability?

And make no mistake: America generates radical subcultures. What are we "conserving" here, after all? A nation of play-it-safe sticks in the mud? Hardly.

III.

Conservatives, myself included, are often drawn to imagery and a tone conveying order and discipline—respectability and reverence—but we too often overlook the tumultuous real history of the nation we are attempting to defend and speak for:

- This is a nation in which, during the Revolutionary period we rightly revere, ad hoc groups of rioting (and frequently drunk) citizens in a given locale, such as the Sons of Liberty, would spontaneously declare themselves a legislature, "mobbing" representatives of the existing colonial governments—*and even post-Revolution governments*—into abandoning enforcement of prior laws.
- This is a nation in which, until the late nineteenth century, virtually *every* white male was a freeholder of independent property and, in effect, a self-employed man (a farmer, normally), as repulsed by the idea of becoming an employee as by the idea of taking orders from kings and politicians. (Much that conservatives defend as traditional is quite newfangled, from the corporation to the nuclear family—not that I am thus condemning these things, merely suggesting that we look deeper to see what really endures and what we're really conserving, while at the same time accepting the potential for mind-bogglingly vast changes and upheavals.)
- This is the nation so opposed to government interference that anti-draft riots burned down significant portions of New York City during the Civil War—not far from where Reed and Cale would live together a hundred years later on the Lower East Side.
- Damn it, it's the nation that invented cowboys and the frontier.
- This is a nation that—without any help from government—invented jazz, flappers, beatniks, bikers, rock 'n' roll, the anarchic punk

movement, and now the roiling and spontaneously communal realm of social networking.

- This is a nation that may even now be rediscovering its roots in "Tea Party" antigovernment activism, tapping into the revolutionary imagery and rhetoric that I've long hoped might one day remind even my fellow New Englanders that they were not always servile before government.

Keep in mind that al Qaeda hates it all, from the hippies to the evangelical Christians to the Hollywood starlets—and there is a sense in which they're being more consistent in their analysis than we are. They have not, to my knowledge, expressed much hatred for Medicare or the Department of the Interior. Nor should they. These are not individualist institutions that threaten to spread, as American pop culture has, around the world—boosting rebellious impulses, from the rock-influenced "Velvet Revolution" that helped fell European Communism to the covert rock concerts of twenty-first-century Iran and Cuba.

I am not suggesting that conservatism should become less conservative. On the contrary, I am suggesting it more enthusiastically embrace the nation it already defends. You want to sell conservatism to youth, not just here but around the world? Don't just sell them peace and security, sell them adventure and risk, of which America once offered plenty.

As *National Review*'s Helen Rittelmeyer urges me to remember, punk is not just individual freedom and easygoing fun but also a toughness that comes from accepting consequences. She relates the third-hand anecdote of a punk who was elbowed in the face at his first concert and then picked up by a concerned stranger—who did not say "Maybe you can sue even though you knew what you were getting into" but rather "You okay? You able to walk? Good, then get back in the pit and punch somebody."

IV.

Maybe conservatives can eke out a few razor-thin electoral victories now and then by, say, co-opting the Dems' love of Medicare or by sounding tougher on a given military issue. But if they really want to win the larger culture war, they need to make the case that an entire forgotten strand of this country's DNA makes us freedom-loving first and foremost—and regulatory not at all. Kids already know instinctively that they can socially organize more efficiently with electronic media, such as Facebook, than by appealing to the National Endowment for the Arts for a grant or by petitioning a Congress member to form a committee. Why not reposition ourselves as the philosophy that speaks to their market-like intuitions and socially organic institutions?

When Michale Graves, the lead singer of the seminal punk band the Misfits, spoke to a gathering of the New York Young Republicans shortly before Bush's reelection (inspiring me to recruit Graves later for one of the monthly debates at Lolita Bar I host on the Lower East Side), he made the point that America producing a band like the Misfits and a flamboyant singer like him would not seem at all incongruous to the rest of the world, including the many immigrants eager to become part of the United States. This kind of creativity, freedom, and borderline insanity is precisely what the world expects of us—and is the reason that substantial portions of the world's young, in particular, still love us, despite the best efforts of socialist intellectuals and fundamentalist cretins. You don't see people who want the freedom to form and enjoy punk bands flocking to Riyadh or Tehran to do it—save to subvert those places from within.

And heretical as it would sound to most punks, it is not just our freedom that makes them possible but also our prosperity and relative comfort. Suburban 1980s youth listening to New Wave songs—essentially punk made palatable by fusion with disco—were exhilarated by themes of alienation and despair even while continuing to get decent grades and reluctantly mow the lawn. Call it hypocrisy, if you like, but it's not such an unhealthy balance.

Freaky-sounding music or odd clothing are not what conservatives who understand America should be fighting. The taxes and regulations that leave us with fewer such wild and unpredictable choices are the real enemy, and they are formidable, requiring our undivided opposition—requiring, indeed, an upsurge of political fusionism in which Americans of all stripes realize how alien these socialist institutions are in a nation built by freaks and mavericks.

V.

I have thus far addressed conservatives, urging them to think a bit more like punks—but I should also address punks, if any are reading this, and urge them, if they have the courage, to think just a bit more like Republicans. You probably think of yourself as a skeptic, perhaps an "iconoclast"—maybe even something of an anarchist. Traditionally, this attitude among punks has meant opposition to consumer culture and advertising. But how well would big government hold up under even a moment of Nietzschean doubt?

If TV is lying to you with its advertisements, what on earth is the government doing when it promises to end poverty or racism? A truly skeptical member of the counterculture should be embarrassed to support politicians who say they can spend our money more effectively than we can—or make us freer with their Byzantine regulations. Surely one can be a punk without thinking that socialist planning would be more liberating than much-maligned suburbia—or that people are made better able to function as fearless individuals by campus speech codes, which were largely fashioned by Leftists (such as the ones I encountered at Brown University, in between living in suburbia and living in Manhattan).

Take a moment away from hating conservatives to remember another of your historic foes: the hippies. Not all countercultures are equal, and it's easy to forget in the fluid, mix-and-match twenty-first century that there were once battle lines drawn between the punk and hippie subcultures (lines that began blurring together in the grunge culture of the 1990s). Though I'd like nothing more than to see all of America's subcultures, the latter-day hippies included, turn against government, there are lessons to be drawn from the reasons punks hated hippies.

While the hippies fancied themselves foes of the Establishment, they whined—as some now do from positions *within* the Establishment—for government to refashion the world to their liking. If only we all believe hard enough, all of us together in a big happy circle, anything is possible, thought the hippies, including a world without evil or an economy without money. Punks, blessed with greater hindsight, greater cynicism, and a healthier dose of aggression, realized that wishing, chanting, and protesting don't necessarily make something so. This is always the first step toward political and philosophical maturity: seeing that reality contains limitations—laws of economics, logic, and science—that cannot be defied willy-nilly.

Punk was, in part, an effort to come to terms with a world that frustrates unrealistic, unworkable plans. Indeed, Johnny Rotten of the Sex Pistols blamed the socialism-induced poverty of early-1970s England for spawning punk—and it took a good deal of its inspiration from the mean streets of New York City during that time, when proto-punk bands such as the Ramones were performing at the club CBGB's.

I ask you to recognize in government's attempts to plan the economy and the culture—and, in recent years, even the weather—another shiny-happy-utopian pile of nonsense. On their (all too rare) good days, at least the Republicans try to shrink government. If we could shrink it to nothing, we'd be making real progress. At the very least, no anarchist—and no one enamored of spontaneous cultural experimentation—should be allied with the bland, boring leviathan in DC, or its tendrils in every state and town in America.

VI.

After all, as a punk—or a conservative, or both—you know you can do things for yourself without waiting for orders and assistance from local authorities. Ask not what your country can do for you but *what you can do for yourself and others willing to interact with you to mutual benefit*. True punks have long known—as members of any vibrant subculture do, to some extent—that you can't wait for the whole world (or even a democratic majority) to catch on to a good idea if you want to see it enacted. You need to *do it yourself*: DIY, as the punks say for short.

The Nobel-winning economist Milton Friedman was beloved on the Right. His son, guided by the same free-market principles, is an anarchist. His grandson, equally market-oriented, is an avid participant in the annual Burning Man festivals held in the desert in Nevada by body-painting, often drug-addled performance artists and sculptors—and he is working on a project to build boats and artificial islands that will function as free sovereign nations. Some might think this is an odd, radical-sounding way for the grandson of Milton Friedman to spend his time, but, obviously, I say: *What could be more American than that?*

It's with good reason we are more inspired, for example, by the Wright Brothers building their own airplane than we are by Congress deciding to funnel billions of dollars from innocent taxpayers into the maw of Lockheed Martin or Boeing. The best way to make the world a better place—and to protect our rights—is to keep government out of the way, a principle understood, in different, fragmented ways, by conservatives like Reagan, who vowed to get government off our backs, and by any punk who's been hassled by cops for dancing in a bar that has no cabaret license (as now happens in New York City with some regularity).

The nation that produced the Ramones and the Misfits, each with at least one conservative member, does not naturally await subsidies and legal decrees. Rather than conservatives running a few more senior citizen focus groups or opinion polls—and struggling, if we're lucky, to get from 46 to 51 percent in the next general election—I suggest we remind Americans who they are, which is a rather unruly and creative bunch of risk-takers. The current period of town hall tumult, not so unlike the days of the Sons of Liberty during the Revolution, is the perfect time to do it. This country carries the potential to become a very different place almost overnight, history suggests—indeed, to do so again and again, and without waiting for approval from Washington.

19

WHY I'M GLAD LIBERALS ARE BULLIES

Ben Shapiro

Ackerman Union at the University of California at Los Angeles is a five-story brick-and-cement structure that overlooks a large swath of the university. The view from the top of Ackerman is pretty—you can see the John Wooden Center to the west, as well as the intramural soccer fields and Pauley Pavilion. To the north is Bruin Walk, a sloping road along which college groups congregate to peddle their ideological wares.

Closest to Ackerman, though, is Bruin Plaza. The plaza itself is exactly what you would expect: an empty brickwork courtyard with a large statue of the college's bear symbol to the northwest, and with a raised stage to the north.

On March 8, 2001, the plaza was packed with students. Rowdy and noisy, sloganeering and chanting, filling up the plaza with sound and bodies. Not just UCLA's black and Hispanic students—junior high and high school students bused in to the university, presumably with their parents' and teachers' permission, to protest the University of California's so-called Standing Policies 1 and Standing Policies 2 (SP-1 and SP-2).

SP-1 and SP-2 were policies adopted by the UC Board of Regents in the lead-up to California's wildly popular Proposition 209, which banned preferential treatment based on race, particularly in college admissions. In short, Prop. 209 banned affirmative action in the UC system, dealing a heavy blow to the "diversity" fanatics who for decades had insisted that skin tone rather than merit be the leading criteria for a UC slot.

SP-1 and SP-2 were somewhat softer than the text of Prop. 209 itself. Those policies supposedly eliminated racial considerations in UC admissions. In fact, SP-1 and SP-2 guaranteed only that 50 to 75 percent of the incoming student body would be admitted based solely on grades and test scores; the other 50 to 25 percent could be admitted based on factors like "special talents" and "academic accomplishments in the context of disadvantaged circumstances." These were not hardheaded color-blind policies, but softer variants.

The immediate effect of SP-1 and SP-2 was a drop in the number of "minority students" admitted to UCLA. This sent the multicultural Left into a frenzy. They immediately began to organize to fight for the repeal of SP-1 and SP-2, no matter the consequences for the intellectual level of the student body. In place of those policies, the Leftists wanted something vaguer, called "comprehensive review"—in essence, sob stories in admissions essays that could subtly signal to admissions officers the socioeconomic status of the applicants.

By 2001, their ire had reached fever pitch. In February 2001, UC professors largely endorsed the repeal of SP-1 and SP-2, releasing a petition decrying the policies, and stating that SP-1 and SP-2 "posted a huge UNWELCOME sign for all black, Latino, and other minority students who want to come to the UC." They went so far as to call the policies "segregation" and "racial inequality . . . that [has] for too long poisoned our national life." Those same professors announced that, on March 8, they would cancel classes, shift their normal courses to teach about the beauties of affirmative action, and tell students to attend rallies as part of a "Day of Action to Reverse the Ban Now."

At the time of the rallies, I had just turned seventeen, and I was still deciding whether I wanted to be a political science major or a philosophy major. I had written a few popular conservative columns for the UCLA daily paper, the *Daily Bruin* (dissenting columns are a rarity at major universities), and I'd confronted some of my professors in class, but I hadn't truly put myself in harm's way. It was all fun and games, basic campus rabble-rousing.

I thought the March 8 rally would provide more of the same—entertaining banter and perhaps even some intelligible discussion.

Which is why I was standing atop Ackerman Union, overlooking Bruin Plaza, with fifteen hundred students standing below me, holding a giant homemade sign reading: MERIT BEFORE DIVERSITY: SAVE SP-1 AND SP-2.

At first, nobody noticed me—I was the only counterprotester. After a few moments, however, some of the members of the crowd—probably high school students cutting class to protest—looked up at me and started shouting. I couldn't hear what they said, but it wasn't hard to read the expressions on their faces. They weren't happy.

Soon more members of the crowd began to turn in my direction, away from the stage. It was like watching a snowball gain momentum—

first a few, then more, then many, then most of them looked up at me and started shouting. Now I could hear them.

"Look at that fool!"

"You son of a bitch!"

It was all talk to me—hell, I'd heard worse than that at my Jewish day school. And besides, the cameras were aimed up at the sign, and that was good—our cause only had me, and media attention would magnify the presence of the opposition disproportionately.

Then I heard someone shouting. And this time, I was scared.

"That asshole! Let's go up there and push him off!"

At that point, I thought it wise to move off the roof of Ackerman. I remember thinking, "It's one thing to stand up for merit—it's another thing to be thrown off a roof for it."

But I was seventeen, and I was too dumb for my own good. So I decided to confront the ralliers firsthand. I climbed down the four stories as fast as I could, then made my way out into the plaza. A reporter from KNX 1070 was there, and I dashed off a few quick thoughts. There was someone from UPN TV, and I spoke to him, too.

That's when some of the ralliers noticed that I was now in their midst. They confronted me quickly, stuck their fingers in my face. Congregated around me. Crushed me in.

Now, I'm no football linebacker at age twenty-six, and at seventeen, I hadn't even finished my growth spurt. I was maybe five foot seven and a hundred and forty pounds. So, figuring that prudence was the better part of valor, I got out of there. But not before quickly calculating where the enormous crowd was going to march. Because, as I said, I was too dumb to know better.

I figured out that they were going to make their slow and steady way through the campus, and that eventually they'd have to walk by the inverted fountain (read: toilet bowl) located where the math/science and liberal arts buildings meet. So I sprinted there and set up shop. I wanted to force each and every one of those protesters to confront the fact that even at UCLA, there were those who would oppose their bully tactics.

Sure enough, about ten minutes later, the crowd came marching up toward the fountain. And there I stood, holding my sign, waiting for them.

At that point, even the rally organizers got scared. The last thing they wanted was footage of their entitlement-mentality thugs beating up a short Jewish kid. So they stationed members of their own rally around me, both shielding me from the crowd and protecting the crowd from my subversive message.

That didn't stop members of the crowd from blustering.

"You racist pig!" one big burly fellow screamed in my face. "Don't you worry, we'll get you later."

"You honky!" shouted another, oblivious to the irony of his racial slur.

In the end, I came away without a scratch, a fact that surprises me even now.

Two months later, the UC Regents bowed to the student, faculty, and staff pressure and rescinded SP-1 and SP-2, and a few months after that, replaced them with "comprehensive review." The effect on the campus population was devastating—SAT scores were made a last priority rather than a first one, SAT-IIs, including Spanish, were elevated, and the victimhood essays (for which each reader was allotted eight to ten minutes per candidate) were made paramount. Unsurprisingly, for the class of 2006, admitted just after the adoption of comprehensive review, 191 students were rejected who had 1,500+ SAT scores, along with another 1,455 with scores 1,410–1,500. Meanwhile, 106 students were admitted with SATs of 810–900, another 412 were admitted with 910–1,000.

So I didn't win.

But I did learn a valuable lesson: fighting makes you stronger. Pressure turns coal into diamonds.

Today's young conservatives are better prepared than their parents, because they have to face liberal bullying on a daily basis, from the elementary-school level through grad school and on into their careers (particularly law, education, and Hollywood). To survive, they learn how to fight back. While their apathetic peers are off drinking beer and figuring out how to parrot arguments back to their professors in order to earn good grades, conservatives are learning liberal arguments inside and out—and learning how to counter them.

More than that, young conservatives are building the intestinal fortitude necessary to fight liberal bullying. The fact is that modern liberalism has fascist roots, and those roots have grown too large for the surrounding soil—the roots are now exposed for everyone to see. Liberals feel free to shut down debate with Alinsky's tactics, slandering their opponents with insulting labels. And too many conservatives in positions of power cave.

Young conservatives don't cave, because they've grown up facing down this tactical tyranny. They've seen it on a near-daily basis. And if they use their time "underground" to hone their skills, they come out of the process sharpened to a razor's edge.

They need that edge, because the total dominance of liberalism in our education system and in our pop culture takes in all of the politically apathetic. It's so easy for members of the apathetic crowd to embrace buzzwords like *multiculturalism* and *diversity* simply for the sake of getting laid or meeting new buddies. But that is why young conservatives do themselves a disservice not to enter the battleground fully armed. We do have the power to help inform the apathetic, and to fight the preconceptions being imbibed by those who simply don't care enough to challenge them. We can't convince our political opponents, but we can swing independents/apathetics into our column.

I know because I've seen it happen. One of the first classes I took at UCLA was called Geography 5. The professor, Joshua Muldavin, was an entertaining fellow who identified himself as a communist, and who said that the Tiananmen Square massacre had been a case of protesters standing up for communism and the Chinese government standing up for capitalism. Over the course of the quarter, I began challenging him in class. Soon there was a group of us willing to ask him tough questions. We all sat together, and he sneeringly called us "Republican Row." By the end of the class, a large swath of the students agreed with us. That would never have happened if we'd been silent.

Young conservatives aren't silent. They're fighters. They stand atop buildings and hold signs and talk to the media. More than that, they look down the barrel of the Leftist revolver—the revolver loaded with bullets marked RACIST, SEXIST, HOMOPHOBE—and say "Go ahead, make my day." Because young conservatives know that the Leftist ammunition, is, in essence, a chimera. Liberals have nothing except bully tactics. Until conservatives look down the barrel of that revolver, they're scared; once they've forced liberals to fire, and once they come out unscathed, they're battle-tested warriors.

So thank God for liberal thugs. They're the people who are going to save this country, by forcing true conservatives to stand up for founding principles fearlessly, without regret, and without hesitation.

20

DUCKING THE COFFINS

How I Became an Edu-Con

Ashley Thorne

"It says here you're from Texas," my interlocutor said. "You don't like Bush, do you?"

"Oh, uh . . . well, does it really matter either way?"

"But you *don't* like him, right?"

It was my first week in New York. Captivated by the glamour of the city and the unorthodox mission of the tiny Christian college I was entering as a freshman, I had gone out hopefully looking for a source of income. This interview took place at a retail children's clothing store on Thirty-fourth Street. I didn't get the job.

My first week in New York and the flop interview coincided with the 2004 Republican National Convention. Delegates inside Madison Square Garden were chanting "Four more years!" while protesters filling the streets of my new neighborhood shouted phrases I couldn't understand. I headed home from the children's store, weaving through gay rights activists and ducking under coffins carried by the marchers.

What was this world I had entered? I came from Dallas, Texas, where everyone I knew really *did* love Bush. Growing up there, I had gone to private classical schools, studied Latin, and learned the Texas state song ("Texas, our Texas, all hail the mighty state!"), which modestly described my homeland as "Boldest and grandest, withstanding ev'ry test, O Empire wide and glorious, you stand supremely blest."

That wide and glorious empire was far away now. I had moved to a blue state; I had moved to New York City.

I came there to go to the King's College, a Christian school in the Empire State Building. I didn't know then that I would meet my future husband that week and that I would stay in the Northeast after college. Today I live in Jersey City, New Jersey, and work as a writer for the National Association of Scholars, an organization seeking to preserve intellectual freedom in American higher education.

One thing that surprised me when I first started at King's was the political enthusiasm of some of my freshman classmates. A group of guys I knew went into the protester-packed streets wearing shirts that read BUSH IS MY HOMEBOY—they said they wanted to get into debates with the Bush-bashers. As part of new student orientation, the college took us on a field trip to the youth section of the RNC. Several from our group spotted news cameras and immediately put themselves forward to be interviewed. It seemed everyone around me felt strongly one way or the other. As for me, I figured I was a Republican, but that was by association with my family and my Texas roots, and other than being against abortion, I really couldn't articulate my political beliefs.

But I liked the feisty spirit at King's College, planted in the heart of New York to be a countercultural force. The college's mission—to prepare students for and plant them in "strategic institutions"—resonated with me. It wasn't a typical Christian college tucked away in a rural town with mandatory chapel and a no-drinking pledge. Nor was it typical of college in general. As a student there, I lived in a mouse-ridden Midtown apartment building with doormen and no thirteenth floor, wore business clothes on campus, and had classes interrupted by terrorism alerts over the Empire State Building intercom.

This felt more authentic—to be "in the world," not apart from it. I wanted to be where ideas were born and where I could have my own nebulous ideas take shape.

Today I identify with the principles of the intellectually conservative movement for which I work. I believe that higher education colors the contact lenses through which we see the world. It can either bestow our civilization's legacy or prompt us to reject that legacy. I saw this illustrated around the breakfast table this past Christmas when my extended family got into a heated discussion over government regulation and one uncle passionately defended farming subsidies and the health-care bill. "How did he get to be so liberal?" my father-in-law asked later. "He went to the University of Maryland," said Grandma.

I, on the other hand, came out of college appreciative of the free market, concerned about big-government initiatives, and wanting to build my life on traditional values. My husband and I hope to populate the earth with a few little conservatives. And my public writing in my job reflects the convictions of people like Allan Bloom, whose *The Closing of the American Mind* sometimes seems like the NAS's Magna Carta. (Not that NASers are generally Platonists or Straussians. They represent a great variety of views, united mostly in opposition to the intellectual imperialism of the Left.) At twenty-three, I am a junior culture warrior learning to take a stand for sound education in an academic world saturated in political correctness and anti-intellectualism. So how did I get to be so conservative, and remain so while living in the heart of the secular liberal Northeast?

The main fortifiers of my beliefs have been my family and my education. Growing up in a Christian missionary family was foundational. My father read the Bible to me during breakfast every morning before school, and my mother instituted a weekly family night on which we would all say something kind to—she called it "honor"—one person at the table.

We went as a family to Russia once or twice a year with my parents' humanitarian aid ministry and visited orphanages, schools, hospitals, and prisons. My first trip was in January of 1995, when Russia was still in the shadow of the Iron Curtain. I remember entering a gray concrete school building and giving a shy Russian girl my best friendly American smile. She looked at me blankly. I later asked my father why she didn't smile back. "After seventy years of Communism in Russia, people don't have much to smile about. They need the hope of Jesus," he told me.

I also went to Cuba as a twelve-year-old on a mission trip for which the Cuban administration had made a special exemption. During the orientation in Mexico, I was instructed not to talk about the government or why we were there—even the hotel phone might be bugged. In Cuba I saw worse poverty than any I had seen in Russia, and I met underground Christians gathering in homes. They offered my group their month's pittance of a meat ration and served a salad topped with vegetables cut to spell DIOS ES AMOR.

Both snowy Russia and sweltering Cuba were covered by the same dark cloud of Communism. My parents wanted me to see this darkness for myself so that I would appreciate the freedom I own as an American.

When I began looking at colleges, King's was their suggestion. Picturing myself studying serenely on a grassy Washington & Lee-esque campus, I had no desire to go to school in cold, metal Gotham. And I thought the King's admissions people too bold asking questions like, "Where do you see yourself in five years? How about ten years?" How should I know? But a visit and a scholarship later, I changed my mind.

On move-in day, there was a sign on my apartment door that said HOUSE OF MARGARET THATCHER. My roommates and I were confused until we learned that King's had created a system in which all students are assigned to one of nine houses, named for conservative or Christian heroes such as Ronald Reagan, Dietrich Bonhoeffer, and Queen Elizabeth I—to the exclusion of such icons as Franklin Delano Roosevelt, Richard Rorty, and John Maynard Keynes.

In a 2005 *National Review Online* article, Stanley Kurtz called King's "a fascinating experiment in higher education—an ultimate encounter of red and blue America." True, the college was made up mostly of conservative Christians, but it wasn't trying to cultivate, like cattails in the Sahara, Republicans in New York. Rather, the experiment was to approach education differently from most American colleges: teaching students to pursue truth—and acknowledging that there is such a thing as truth in the first place, though finding it was not presumed to be easy or simple.

My major at King's was modeled after one at Oxford: Politics, Philosophy, and Economics (PP&E). It was a liberal arts program that began with Plato and Aristotle and ended with a senior thesis. Down in the basement of the Empire State Building, I sweated over microeconomics charts and heard for the first time that "there ain't no such thing as a free lunch," an unfortunate truth to find out for a college student living in the most expensive city in the country. I took Philosophical Apologetics from Peter Kreeft, a nimble seventy-year-old Catholic philosopher dedicated to the writings of Socrates and the seasons of the Boston Red Sox. The final exam for that class was to write sixty arguments for the existence of God.

I took rhetoric—better labeled Learning to Write through Mortification—from my current boss Peter Wood, then the provost of the college. For the class, we wrote op-ed–style papers on current events. We had to use a five-syllable word in the first sentence—an exercise aimed at making us slow down and think about the exact words we were using—and were graded on our use of metaphor and "imaginative realization." Each week we had to integrate a new figure of speech, such as a zeugma, enallage, or aposiopesis. The class was called rhetoric, as in the classical art of using language to persuade, not the modern connotation of obscuring the truth. The syllabus said:

> *The art of persuasive writing can and often is put to bad use, in efforts to justify unworthy behavior and misguided political agendas. In that sense, this course differs dramatically from rhetorical communication courses as they are taught in many colleges and universities. This is not a course in how to shade the truth, to lie with statistics, or to persuade people against their better judgment. To the contrary, it is a course in how to persuade people to improve their judgment and to listen to reasonable counsel.*

In class we had to project our papers on a screen and read them out loud to our classmates. Dr. Wood asked each person to give a critical comment (no positive remarks allowed) and coaxed us, with Socratic method, to talk about whether the word "dogged" worked in a metaphor calling Harriet Myers a pit bull, or whether the paper had succeeded in its aim. It was a humbling class; my first paper earned a whopping 43. And it wasn't easy, listening to my friends and professor pointing out the mixed metaphors, lack of evidence, and poor word choice in my writing. But rhetoric taught me the importance of words, sentences, and figures of speech in formulating an argument.

For my senior thesis, I examined the permissibility of abortion for pregnancies caused by rape. I analyzed Judith Jarvis Thompson's "Defense of Abortion" and considered reasons why conservative politicians typically make the rape exception. My advisor was David Tubbs, a true scholar who taught Statesmanship with Shakespeare plays and Public Policy with texts by Robert George, Hadley Arkes, and Rochelle Gurstein. His seminars prompted me to think about some of the biggest policy issues of our time. When I wasn't secretly tallying the number of times he asked someone in the class to "Be more specific," I weighed various arguments for reparations, the implications of legislating morality, Captain Vere's decision to execute Billy Budd, and whether a nonreligious case could be made against gay marriage.

In all my courses, professors urged the class to compare competing arguments and seek the most accurate one, to see ideas in the context of the historical whole. Conservatism was never forced on us, and I know people who have graduated from King's as hippies, Democrats, or staunch libertarians believing that God is a free-market capitalist. For me, the texts I read and the concepts I thought about in college reinforced some of my beliefs, knocked others to smithereens, and gave me some new ones.

And just keeping up with the pace of my course load was a struggle. You get out of college what you put into it, and I surely could have gained more by working harder and actually reading everything assigned to me (I didn't). Running around the city on nannying jobs and spending time with friends and my future husband were welcome diversions. I know I have much more to learn. King's, too, had its limitations, with only two majors, one sporting event per year, and an enrollment small enough that the entire school knew who you were. Like other students there, I inevitably wondered what it would be like to go to college somewhere else. Yet I stayed.

I was meeting with Dr. Tubbs for my thesis one day when he told me that Peter Wood, who had earlier that year left King's for the National Association of Scholars, was looking to hire someone and wondered if I was interested in an interview. I went home, looked up the NAS, and read that it was a Princeton-based organization that fights political correctness in higher education.

King's and my primary education had kept me sheltered from the liberal worldview projected in most classrooms. I was never taught that the universe came about through evolution. I was never taught that global warming was real. I was never taught that capitalism was exploitative, that America was an oppressive society, that I was a racist because I was white, or that I should reexamine my heterosexuality. I'd heard the ideas; they just didn't make much of an impression. My schools never passed out condoms, asked me to consider being a Safe Zone ally, or taught me how to calculate my carbon footprint. I never read *Beloved*, *Silent Spring*, *Nickel and Dimed*, or *A People's History of the United States*. I never watched *An Inconvenient Truth* or *Fahrenheit 9/11*. These films and books may all be excellent in their own way, and perhaps I'll get around to them one of these days, but first on my list are *Love's Labour's Lost*, *Anna Karenina*, and G. K. Chesterton's *Orthodoxy*.

I hadn't experienced the liberal campus for myself—although I got a sample the day of my interview on 34th Street—but because of what I *had* learned, I could see why it didn't fit in with higher education. I had learned about the great thinkers and principles of politics, philosophy, and economics. I had been to Russia and Cuba and seen for myself the bitter inheritance Communism bequeathed to those countries. And I had studied debates over the right to privacy, racial preferences, and freedom of expression. I was already aligned with the NAS's values and had practically lived its vision of the ideal university.

I went to Princeton for an interview and got the job this time. Within the next month, I graduated from King's, got married, moved across the Hudson to Jersey City, and started my first real-world job.

One of my first assignments at NAS was to write the story of Bill Felkner, a social work student at Rhode Island college who faced years of persecution on account of his political views as a libertarian. Having attained a bachelor's degree in psychology at the college, and encouraged by one of his professors, Felkner began pursuing a master's degree in social work. In his first semester in the School of Social Work, he wrote a class paper arguing against a social welfare bill. The assignment was to advocate for the bill, but Felkner trusted that he would still be graded fairly no matter what position he took. But his trust was in vain: his professor gave him an F accompanied by the comment, "Regardless of the content, application of theory, and critical analysis, you did not write from the perspective you were required to use in this academic exercise. Therefore, the paper must receive a failing grade."

In the same semester, Felkner objected to the School of Social Work's promoting the film *Fahrenheit 9/11*, including showings in social work classes. He e-mailed his professor to point out that the film was politically biased and that it had nothing to do with social work. The professor wrote this in reply:

> *I revel in my biases. So, I think that anyone who consistently holds antithetical views to those that are espoused by the profession might ask themselves whether social work is the profession for them.*

Felkner also met with the chair of the bachelor social work program, who told him, "We hope that all social workers are liberal."

Writing this article and talking with Bill, I had my first encounter with the ugly side of higher education—one that tries to shut out all who decline to cheerlead for the Left's agenda. I've learned since then that universities love to pitch their tent on misleading terms, such as "diversity," meaning special privileges for people in particular identity groups; "social justice," meaning advocacy of state-sponsored redistribution; "global citizenship," meaning hatred of America; and "sustainability," meaning anti-capitalism and population control in the name of environmentalism.

My generation goes to college mainly because it's culturally accepted as the natural next step after high school. College is, for us, a transition from living at home, a place to play, and a time to grow up. Most of us don't really know what we want to get out of college (friends? memories? vocational skills?) and we just hope to find some sort of niche where we feel comfortable. But college has the power to be so much more than this—to crystallize ideas and make us who we are.

The content in which we invest—books, lectures, conversations, extracurricular involvements, declarations by those in authority—shapes how we view the world. Of course, not everyone automatically adopts the perspectives of their college. Many people I've talked with, like Bill Felkner, resist the culture of conformity to progressive politics. For instance, I've gotten to know Sylvia Wasson, a warm and fearless woman who teaches German language at Santa Rosa Junior College in California. After she spoke out against her college's clandestine efforts to put racial preferences (illegal in California's public institutions) into policy on her campus, she was labeled a troublemaker and a racist. The college commissioned an investigative report vilifying Professor Wasson and made it available for public viewing. She remains disfavored at her college for challenging its subversive endeavors to install racial preferences.

There are others I have talked with via e-mail, such as Margaret Matthews (not her real name), an assistant director of student affairs at a university in the South. She contacted me asking for advice on how to document the folly of her university's commitments to "diversity." She wrote an article for NAS telling about a meeting she had with the vice president of student affairs. In the meeting, she asked to transfer to a new department and was told there would be difficulty "finding another black woman to replace you." Matthews had hoped to use her expertise in an area other than the office of multicultural affairs, but she had already been labeled. "There I was, just one person sitting there, but she was seeing a group."

I also know Bill Rivers, a boyish-looking, articulate honors student at the University of Delaware. He was astounded when he had to participate in a mandatory freshman residence life program that aimed to teach ideological lessons about racism and oppression. In one session, Rivers recalled, students were told to write down all the racial epithets and slurs they could think of. Instead of bringing the white freshmen to repentance for their biases, the exercise only embarrassed everyone and caused them to focus more on racial stereotypes than they otherwise would have. Rivers told his professor Jan Blits, the head of the NAS Delaware affiliate, about the program, and Professor Blits worked with the Foundation for Individual Rights in Education to gather documentation and expose the program. The University of Delaware president immediately shut down the program.

Bill Felkner, Sylvia Wasson, Margaret Matthews, Bill Rivers, Jan Blits, and people like them are my heroes. Like boulders in a hurricane, they remain unmoved in their convictions, even if they face retaliation for doing so. If I had gone to a secular university, I hope I would have had courage like theirs. Their stories make me grateful that I never had to make a choice between compromising my beliefs and being bullied for expressing them.

Yes, the 34th Street retail-store manager didn't look too kindly on me when he suspected I liked President Bush. But I never faced discrimination in college. Perhaps that store manager inadvertently gave me a push toward my becoming self-consciously conservative. He started me on the path to the realization that the affinities we feel, the choices we make, and the ideas we entertain reverberate in the wider cultural atmosphere. We can let that happen through happenstance—avoiding unpromising confrontations and practicing the equivalent of ducking under the coffins carried by protesters on 34th Street. Or we can make thoughtful choices about when and how to speak up.

An all-too-frequent "entertainment" at the corner of 34th Street and Fifth Avenue was a guy with an assortment of plastic buckets. He would set up his own drumming exhibition, taking advantage of the canyon formed by the Empire State Building and adjacent buildings. His clunking message got plenty of amplification. What was that message? I suspected it was mostly to the storeowners, and was something like, "Pay me and I'll move my concert somewhere else."

Speaking up for the sake of making a noise, attracting attention because you can, banging on plastic buckets—adding to the cultural cacophony—is not the kind of reverberation I would like to make. But if I can help bring attention to Bill Felkner's fight against his "I-revel-in-my-biases" professor, or the attempt of Santa Rosa Junior College to smear Sylvia Wasson, or Margaret Matthews's thwarted hopes, that's something. Conservatives need to conserve a lot of things. One of them is a decent sense of how to convey worthy grievance. The great model for that is the Declaration of Independence, but I am mindful, too, of the many smaller models of people standing up, at some personal risk, to local tyrannies. Higher education has been too long conceded by mainstream conservatives to the Left, and it has consequently grown into a world where the Left often rules with such florid arrogance that George III himself would have been embarrassed. I see in the university an institution that is far too important to our civilization to surrender to these folks. That's what I'm trying to conserve.

21

PROSPERITY

The Choice of a New Generation

Michael Warren

There's a chilling idea going around these days that America is losing its edge. We outsource all our labor to Asia, for instance, and our health care costs are going up. Despite our election of Berlin's favorite president, America's standing with the other nations of the world seems worse than ever. Unemployment rates are hanging out at thirty-year-high levels. The surprise television hit of 2009 (though is it really a surprise?) was MTV's *Jersey Shore*.

And yet, America's prospects have never looked better.

I'm not joking when I say that. Folks like Thomas Friedman may believe we're in the midst of a dawning Chinese century, but it's much more likely that the twenty-first will follow the twentieth as a distinctly American century. Progressive liberals certainly hope and many conservatives certainly fear that the United States is inching or even walking briskly toward European-style social democracy—but that's not likely, either.

As a member of the so-called Millennial Generation, I may have the most reason to believe that my country's place as a leader in innovation and inspiration is a relic of the past. After all, I'm about to graduate from college into a terrible labor market as mounds of generational debt is voted upon me. I've been frightened into thinking that every time I buy a burrito at Taco Bell, the Earth is going to get its sweet revenge by flooding my house and/or burning me to a crisp. I also have to worry about AIDS, swine flu, secondhand smoke, carbon-monoxide poisoning, and any of the million other ways I am going to die. To make matters worse, the soundtrack to this disastrous state is Lady Gaga—and I think I'm even beginning to like Lady Gaga. This can't bode well for another age of American prosperity. Can it?

It took living over three months in the modern utopia of the European Union for me to confirm that things aren't so bad here in the States. In fact, they're quite good. This generation has the opportunity, not to mention the ability, of building on the institutions and advances of past American generations to create and sustain a vibrant and free society, if we choose to do so. Certainly there's something about the institutions of the United States that engenders success and wealth. We have fewer regulations and more liberal tax laws than many Western countries, characteristics that make our country more amenable to entrepreneurism and experimentation.

There's also a cultural element to American success, which I did not fully appreciate before my time abroad. British columnist Melanie Phillips, writing in the *Daily Mail*, referred to the United States as a nation "that still believes in itself." This, she says, is opposed to the

United Kingdom, where there exists "hostility to the country's identity and values." The same, perhaps, could be said for many other European countries. My own experience living in the Republic of Ireland showed me one of the most disappointing cases of this national ennui in Europe. Ireland also provides one of the better cautionary tales for my generation, which sits at a societal crossroads of sorts.

I spent a semester at the National University of Ireland in Galway. In many ways, life for a student in Ireland isn't much different from life in the United States. Students go to class (or skip it) with perhaps the same frequency as those in America. The central dining hall houses both a Subway sandwich chain and an environmentally friendly, fair-trade, guilt-free coffee shop called Eco-Grounds, which wouldn't be out of place at any university in the States. And the freshmen are always getting lost.

Ireland largely embraces American youth culture. Girls wear their imported Abercrombie and Fitch shirts and sweatpants, while the lads sport gel-infused spiky hairstyles. Walk by the student apartments on any afternoon and you are guaranteed to see either *Friends* or *The Simpsons* on the TV. Were it not for these slightly anachronistic styles and shows (not to mention the delightful brogue), the seaside college town of Galway could easily be mistaken for Ann Arbor or Chapel Hill. Irish students may be about ten years behind us pop-culturally, but they're almost as American as Americans are.

Understanding their culture at a deeper level, however, requires a look back at the history of the republic. Ireland's long road to independence produced a very different national culture than what we Americans have had. Unlike during the American fight for independence, when patriots sought to establish a limited government in place of British tyranny, Irish republicans simply were looking to replace a British government with an Irish one. The philosophical underpinnings of the Irish Free State and the eventual Republic of Ireland were less pronounced than those in the Declaration of Independence and the U.S. Constitution. Importantly, the Anglo-American political tradition was not particularly welcome. Political influences like Catholic corporatism and agrarianism, as well as the politics of unification with the North, excluded Ireland early on from the mid-twentieth-century economic growth of Western Europe. Into the 1980s, Ireland's economy was still largely agrarian and poor, with high corporate tax rates and little homegrown industry to speak of.

This changed after 1987, when the elected political coalition, influenced certainly by the liberal free market successes in the United Kingdom and the United States, made some radical changes toward smaller government. Most important, Ireland lowered its corporate tax rates dramatically, a move that brought foreign direct investment into the country. Foreign companies like Intel relocated major parts of their production to the once-provincial island. The wealth that flowed into Ireland created more disposable income for Irish citizens, so much so that Ireland became one of the wealthiest nations per capita in the European Union. This economic boom, labeled the Celtic Tiger, moved Ireland into the modern world, an achievement that very few believed possible; among the most pessimistic the Irish themselves, who had been dealing with the violence in Northern Ireland and the dead-end nature of a mostly agricultural economy.

The new Ireland has cell phones, grocery and department stores, SUVs, satellite television, and Starbucks. This may be the joint nightmare of traditional preservationists and the opponents of corporate imperialism, but Ireland is a demonstrably better place to live than it was twenty years ago. The march of economic progress may seem obvious and inevitable in the United States, but for the Irish people a generation ago, it took a conscious choice to liberalize.

And therein lies the cultural conflict for the Irish Millennials. For most of their lives, quality of life has improved dramatically at seemingly little cost to them. Their youth was spent so deep in the heart of the Celtic Tiger era that its existence is almost an afterthought. Only now, after banking scandals and a real estate bust far worse than that in the United States, the Irish economy is hitting its biggest slump since the initial boom. The big cars and fast food and modern conveniences aren't going away, but everyone in Ireland recognizes they just don't have the same amount of money in their pockets as they used to. What's disheartening is that this generation may fail to appreciate the ideas that allowed their society to progress while blaming those ideas for their economic problems.

The reaction of the whole of Ireland, including the youth, to the economic downturn has been quite disappointing. After two decades of some of the most liberal economic policies in the European Union, the citizens of Ireland voted "yes" on the Lisbon Treaty, guaranteeing deeper integration of the Irish economy with that of Europe. For Ireland, this means an influx of money through transfer payments from the European Union's coffers. The treaty also promises more industry regulations and will probably force Ireland to raise its corporate tax levels to European Union's standards, measures that will tear away at the country's competitive advantage. All this Ireland chose for itself, after rejecting it sixteen months before, in the first Lisbon Treaty referendum. And one of the most prominent demographic groups to make the swing from "no" to "yes" were youth voters.

What was the rationale for voting on a treaty that would diminish Ireland's advantage in the marketplace (not to mention her national sovereignty)? Most of the students I spoke with about it agreed that it "just seemed like the thing to do." Concerned about their economic well-being, integration with the behemoth European Union is associated with security. The recession that hit between the referenda served as a warning sign of what was to come, and no one wanted to take any chances. After all, the country, as was repeated countless times by the Irish media, was "bankrupt."

The Irish may have sided with business and entrepreneurs on the first vote, but the second vote was clearly in line with what the Irish government wanted. Declan Ganley, an Irish businessman who led the charge against the Lisbon Treaty, was derided as an "eejit" and much worse, and more than one person suggested to me that he was probably a stooge for the Brits or the CIA! Ganley's message was that Irish business would suffer in the overregulated, overtaxed economic environment of a post-Lisbon European Union. Moreover, he and the "no" side of the vote stressed that the republic was essentially giving up its sovereignty to a governmental entity in Brussels. For this, he was accused of being anti-Europe and anti-Irish.

All the technical aspects of the Lisbon Treaty aside, the issue of sovereignty is perhaps the most fundamental part of Irish society that young people have trouble reconciling, because it is linked with national identity. It may seem counterintuitive, given the legendary reach of Irish nationalism, but modern Ireland seems to be bathing in contradiction. The Irish have historically prided themselves on being distinctly un-British—even though they watch just as much British television as they do American. Ireland has forever been one of the most solidly Catholic nations in Europe, even into the twenty-first century—except that hardly any young people attend mass on a regular basis, mostly because the clergy sex abuse scandals have left the

Church in Ireland a shambles. The Irish government has taken great care to preserve the Irish language—despite the reality that most Irish students hated learning the old Gaelic language and only small communities on the coast speak it regularly. A friend once told me that the Irish were so bad at sports that they made up their own and were finally good at something, until Ireland's Gaelic football team began competing annually against Australia's similar Australian football team—and losing.

At the same time, the robust economy and ripe environment for investment and innovation that had come to define modern Ireland has met its apparent demise. Sure, Dublin stands with the best of modern cities in Europe and America, but the closing of factories across Munster and Connacht and a shattered banking system revealed to the Irish youth that perhaps nothing was underneath the prosperity with which they had become so familiar. Old Ireland is gone, and new Ireland is broken, and don't we really need the European Union (and the European Union's money) to get us out of this rut? It's the subconscious but very obvious belief among the Irish, particularly among the youth. It's been a long journey from the self-determination of Michael Collins and Eamon de Valera and a quick abandonment of the moderate move to freer markets and smaller government.

So where's the lesson for Americans, and why are we in a much better position to emerge from this crisis more energized and more prosperous than before? Mark Steyn asks, "What is the energy in a society?" and answers that it's "young people." Young people are in movies, on TV, starting companies, developing ideas, researching at universities, serving in the military, consuming, and investing. And in the United States, the youth are energized and ready to build a better, stronger society, even if we don't know it yet.

The American identity is innovation, and we Millennials still belong to that identity. Americans love to explore the process of trial and error, from souping up their muscle cars to building their own supercomputers. We've been served by a government and a society that tolerates failure in the name of discovery. Even better, this generation has come of age in an open-source era, where technology and ideas are free for experimentation. Steve Jobs may have spent years creating the iPhone, but soon after its release there were college students across the country developing new applications that Apple probably never thought possible. This generation is eager to adapt new platforms to their own creative purposes. While YouTube is a timewaster's mecca and an unending source of funny feline videos, it's also a free, easy-to-use method of content distribution for entrepreneurial types. Brandon Hardesty, a young actor based in California, has uploaded over fifty video clips of his quirky "reenactments" of famous movie scenes onto YouTube. The exposure from these videos has raised his profile in Hollywood and earned him parts in movies. His method is uniquely modern and American, taking advantage of his talents and technology to market himself. These individual examples may not seem like enough, but these smaller innovations and successes will be what continues to build and maintain our economy and livelihood.

Ours is an economy of individuals choosing how to spend their time, money, and resources. Young voters may have caught the Obama fever, but we won't be pleased with the attempts at central planning when they restrict our choices. Our consumption is based on choice, right down to the very last detail. We don't have to buy entire albums anymore; we can pick and choose which songs we want to pay for and download. We can customize our shoes online, picking the color and design, and have them shipped to our doors in days. We aren't even satisfied with the litany of available ringtones on our cell phones, insisting on downloading our own favorite songs or sounds for every person in our contacts list. We young Americans have stopped letting corporations make these important decisions for us, so why will we put up with the government telling us which doctor to go to, or what kind of car to drive?

Ultimately, though, our decision to continue the American tradition of innovation, experimentation, and success will require us to know and appreciate that tradition. We can choose to carry on the tradition in our modern way, or we can slip down a path that leads us to dependency on a bigger government. That is, of course, the flip side to this Millennial coin. If our lives have been marked by rapid technological and communication progress, they've also been subject to attitudes that reinforce dependency. Professors at my university in the United States bemoan the lack of self-sufficiency among many of their students. Students are more likely to ask for the answer than seek advice for how to reach the answer themselves, they say. Some combination of the "push 'em through" mentality of public schools and the cult of self-esteem probably contribute to this. The danger for our generation is not that we will overthrow the establishment for one more to our liking, but that we will expect the establishment to provide for us all the solutions.

Where America has the advantage is in those institutions and traditions that have sustained one of the oldest nations in the world. Ireland is not so fortunate. A victim of the entrenched feudal system in Europe and its own self-immolation by refusing to co-opt the capitalist traditions of its hated British neighbors, the Emerald Isle does not have the institutions from which to gain inspiration and fortitude. Fortunately, we do.

We have the history to justify our existence and our institutions, and our connection to that history is what allows us to believe in ourselves as a nation. We've borne witness to the positive effect that a free and open society can have on its citizens, especially when individuals are able to pursue their own self-interest. As young Americans, the energy of our society, we have to choose to acknowledge both the opportunities we have in a modern world and the economic history from which we have grown.

Perhaps there's a silver lining to this untimely recession. Instead of spending these first years of our adult lives mulling around in self-discovery, the Millennials will be forced to look outward and evaluate the path ahead. Do we want to be saddled with debt, or do we want the work we do over the course of our careers to pay for something more worthwhile than a bloated government making empty promises? Do we want to abandon our identity as a free, prosperous, and advanced nation, or do we choose to strengthen that identity by working harder and by thinking more critically? Do we retreat from this challenge to our way of life, or do we face it with a renewed sense of purpose?

It's all up to the choices we make, as young people and as Americans. I think we'll make the right choice.

22

READING RAND

Discovering the Right to Fail

Joi Weaver

When I was a child, my sister and I frequently participated in statewide church talent competitions: kids would compete in areas like choir, solos, puppet routines, and other artistic endeavors. We trained for months in Bible quizzing: learning verses, trying to see the book as a whole, understanding context. To put it bluntly, we were good at it: we often took the top prizes in our divisions at the state competition. One year, the trophies for the top places were quite large. I was so excited to receive my trophy. I'd worked for months to compete, and felt that I'd certainly earned it.

As our group packed up to go home, I saw another girl from my church walk by, carrying one of the large trophies. She hadn't won any of the top spots, and I wondered how she had ended up with one of the grand trophies. I found out later that there were some trophies left over after the award ceremony, and her mother had bought her a trophy so she wouldn't feel left out. I realized that while she and I would always know which one of us had excelled, no one who saw our trophies on a shelf would know that one of them was empty.

This incident, and others like it, continued to bother me throughout my childhood and high school years. I was irritated when my own efforts at excellence were not rewarded, but was also one of the first to shout "unfair!" when excellence was noted in others. I had great visions of what I might do in the future, ways in which I might "change the world," as I and my peers had so often been told we would. I had no particular plans as to how I should educate myself to make this grand impact, nor any notion that this kind of excellence would involve any particular self-discipline on my own part. Surely someone would soon discover my phenomenal intellect and set me loose in the world!

My generation has been one of the most privileged in history, and, without a doubt, one of the most coddled. Most of us, from the time we were very young, have been told that we could do anything we wanted: become pilots, professional ball players, even presidents. Regardless of outcome, we have been given gold stars and applause for every tiny effort. We were often reminded that sportsmanship mattered more than winning, and that everyone was special. I cannot count the number of times I have heard the phrase "All that matters is that you tried." Surely effort matters a great deal, but for a significant portion of the American public, effort has become the very measure of success. To our great disadvantage, we have generally been made to believe that we were the most talented and skilled individuals ever to grace the planet.

Some of this is due to a change in the perception of rights. The Declaration of Independence states that we are "endowed by [the] Creator with certain inalienable rights." Whether one believes that rights originate from a creator or from natural law, the difference between the contrasting views of our society is that conservatives at least agree that rights are a reflection of essential human nature. One can be secure in his own personhood, while still feeling the spur of pride goading him onward to better performance. If rights are innate, then failure is an acceptable risk, since it doesn't affect the nature of the person who has failed. The more progressive view, on the other hand, insists that human nature is always in flux and can be fundamentally reshaped by education and training. In this view, rights are not innate to human nature (since there is no constant human nature), but are granted by the state, and are enacted with a view toward a measurable equality of outcome.

This latter view is currently the more prevalent, and has had a disastrous effect on an entire generation. If rights are merely granted as a measure of equality, and someone has a less than equal outcome, it must be because they have not been granted their full rights. Every effort must be counted as a success, or the person risks being seen as less than equal. Failure is not an option, in this case, because to fail means to become less than human. Therefore, if someone tells you that you have failed or somehow not measured up to the expected standard, it is a personal attack on one's equality rather than a simple evaluation of behavior and skill.

This attitude is on display on nearly every reality TV show. When a contestant, often in his mid-twenties, is kicked off a show for failing to display the necessary level of skill, he protests, "You just don't understand me, I'm better than everyone here!" Though the viewers mock the presumptuousness of the youth, this delusion should not come as a surprise. Most people under the age of thirty have been inundated with the notion that their self-esteem is the primary concern of everyone around them, and no one else has the right to tamper with this esteem. Self-esteem is promoted as one of the modern cardinal virtues, self-esteem unlinked from any drive for excellence or necessity to achieve.

This attitude eliminates the need for personal ambition and drive, not to mention the discipline and patience to achieve one's dreams. All that matters is that each person learns to "believe in himself." Personal achievement is measured in terms of how one feels about himself, rather than any knowledge gained, skills mastered, or wealth created.

So how does someone raised to believe that she was exceptional, that she would change the world just by being herself, finally come to appreciate the necessity of hard work, the uneven distribution of talent, and find the ability to risk failure? Many young conservatives have come to this point through other ways, but for me, it began when I discovered the novels of Ayn Rand.

I first picked up *Atlas Shrugged* in high school, after becoming entranced with the Rush album *2112* and being informed that it was based on the writings of Rand. The book made a profound impact on me, though not for the reasons that many others in previous generations found her philosophy attractive.

Dagny Taggart and Hank Reardon immediately captured my imagination. I had never read a book with characters who acted and spoke like they did. (It is likely that this is because no one actually talks like Ayn Rand characters except Ayn Rand fans, but that is a topic for another time.) The sheer force of Dagny Taggart's will to succeed, even as the "moochers" gained ever more control over her circumstances, was fascinating—I read the story ravenously, wondering if she would finally triumph over the forces of the unexceptional that surrounded her.

But even more than the characters, I found myself engrossed in the scenes set among the "men in Washington," the string-pullers who orchestrated deals to keep various companies from failing while placing heavier restrictions on the few real producers left in the nation. Who were these people, I wondered, who couldn't see that these companies couldn't produce and should be left to bear the consequences? Who were these people so determined to wipe out any sign of excellence, to the point of destroying any individual who showed any signs of being exceptional? Worse yet, why had I heard some of their arguments coming out of my own mouth?

Discovering Rand's writing is a common experience for many conservatives, but the reasons behind Rand's influence may be different for the upcoming generation of thinkers. For many in earlier generations, Rand's defense of the free market was the charm that drew them into conservatism. But I had been raised in a very conservative home, working part-time from my early childhood all the way through high school, raising my own money for many of my activities and hobbies. I was never drawn toward socialism, and though I appreciated Rand's capitalism, it wasn't what made the greatest impact on me. Nor did her sexual and social morality attract me. I have always been a social conservative, and her ideal interaction between men and women in society left me cold. There was no draw for me in that.

So what was it about Rand that set my mind on fire and changed my path in life? It was her valuation, one might even say worship, of excellence. This was something I had not encountered in such a pure form before. I had become lured into the mind-set of my generation, that everyone was equally special in the same way, and that if someone excelled, it was due to better conditions, or luck, or some other circumstance. I was firmly convinced that others succeeded in life because they had better conditions than I did, and that if I simply had what they had, I could do what they did.

Rand shattered that illusion, and revealed the streak of envy that was embedded in my own heart, and the hearts of most of my generation. We do not strive for excellence—after all, haven't our teachers and parents told us we are perfect just the way we are? —but we desire to have the benefits of excellence, in the name of "fairness." My generation is accustomed to getting a gold star for any amount of effort, and to being told that participation is more important than winning. Our teachers may have meant well, but the lesson most of us learned was to despise and distrust excellence. Rand's stories were something of a shock to my system, revealing the nature of my dislike of those who were more successful than I. Ayn Rand provided the antidote to the poison of a coddling, "self-esteem"–centered culture, and this may prove to be her main value to young conservatives.

Learning to admire excellence was not easy. I had to keep a close watch on my mind, and take note every time I began to think, "They're not so special. If I just had that money, or that job, or that education, I could do everything they do." But, of course, I was reluctant to truly excel, because I had become afraid to risk failure and thus afraid to truly succeed. After all, there can be no excellence without the risk of failure, as Rand showed in her fictional corporations, sheltered from the results of their own inefficiency and lack of skill.

Unfortunately, young conservatives are not immune from this poisonous attitude, despite other indicated leanings toward free-market capitalism, personal responsibility, and other more traditionally conservative ideals. Many a social network and action group has been formed by individuals eager to make a name for themselves and reluctant to lend their skills to an existing group. Internecine fighting has split many a promising group as egos battled to be recognized as the Next Big Thing among young conservatives.

One of the greatest rights has been essentially denied to my generation: the right to fail. We have been coddled and insulated, given a gold star for every project, and never allowed to really fall flat on our faces. Failure is one of the most effective teachers in life; I never understood how to write until I wrote a great many things that simply did not work. I had to be willing to write unreadable pieces for years, and to acknowledge that such efforts were unreadable, before I learned enough to produce something that might be worth reading. Those years of failure and frustration were the best writing teacher I could have asked for. But during that time, and even now, there are those who have insisted on seeing my writing as remarkable and exceptional, and have encouraged me to join in those judgments, even when I knew them to be untrue. When I decline to see my work in quite such a favorable light, they become even more adamant, as if to see my work as less than stellar would be in some way a reflection on my own personal worth.

It is an odd thing, to have to fight to fail, but it is necessary for those who grew up with the constant mantra of "you are special, you are perfect the way you are, always be true to yourself." Failure is an important part of life. Failure teaches us where we are weak, where we are ignorant, where we simply did not try as hard as we might have. To deny someone the right to fail is to deny him the experience of picking himself up and trying again, and finally fighting through to success. Even then, effort and discipline do not guarantee a spot at the top—too few people even in the conservative tradition are willing to play second fiddle to anyone else. The work is no longer seen as the important thing; instead, everyone struggles to become the recognizable face of some new movement or action group. Too many prefer to see themselves as the next Dagny Taggart, instead of taking a clear look at their actual efforts and talents. Everyone wants to be John Galt and no one is willing to be the faithful right-hand man Eddie Willers. Many times during the course of the novel, Dagny expresses her frustration on no longer being able to find good, reliable men to work the everyday jobs that keep her railway running. Those unglamorous jobs are crucial to the success of any endeavor, but too few modern activists are willing to take them on. If they cannot be the pinnacle of excellence themselves, they do not wish to acknowledge it in anyone else, or subject themselves to the vision of another.

The right to fail is an essential part of the fundamental conservative principle and basic human nature that tells us every man has the right and duty to make his own way in the world without depending on anyone else—be it a parent, a teacher, or the state—to smooth his way from cradle to grave. If we do not have the right to fail, then the state is justified in swooping in to "fix" any life that has hit a bumpy patch in the road.

Reading Rand was a hard lesson in learning to recognize the areas of my life in which I had failed to succeed, but it set me on the path of learning to love excellence. It was not pleasant to see myself in the faces of the "moochers," decrying excellence in the name of a false equality, but doing so was the only way to begin to leave that worldview behind, and start learning to make my own way. Failure is no more avoidable than gravity: one does not fly by denying gravity but by acknowledging its existence, and learning the laws that allow one to rise above it.

CONTRIBUTORS

MATTHEW LEE ANDERSON has been observing the intersection of evangelicalism, culture, and politics at MereOrthodoxy.com since 2004, and is the author of *Body Matters: Overcoming the New Gnosticism of Young Evangelicals* (forthcoming Bethany House, 2011).

JOSEPH ASHBY is a frequent contributor to AmericanThinker.com and has been featured on Rush Limbaugh's and Mark Levin's radio programs. He works as an aerospace engineer in Kansas, where he lives with his wife and three children.

ROBIN DEMBROFF is a student in the Torrey Honors Institute at Biola University, graduating with degrees in philosophy and humanities in May 2011. She is a contributing editor for EvangelicalOutpost.com, and has been recognized for her work in fiction and poetry.

MICHAEL BRENDAN DOUGHERTY is a contributing editor at the *American Conservative*. His work has appeared in *The Awl*, *Washington Monthly*, *Politico*, the *New Pantagruel*, the *Guardian*, and on ComedyCentral .com. He is a 2009–2010 Phillips Journalism Fellow.

Originally from Wilmington, Delaware, **ANDREW FOY** is a medical resident at Thomas Jefferson University Hospital in Philadelphia, Pennsylvania, as well as an author and writer. His work has appeared in the AmericanThinker.com. He attended medical school at Jefferson Medical College and received his undergraduate training from Ursinus College, where he graduated with honors in biochemistry and molecular biology.

NATHAN HARDEN is a journalist, musician, and author. He blogs about higher education at *National Review* online, and has written for *National Review*, *The Huffington Post*, and many other publications. He graduated from Yale in 2009.

A carpenter by day, **JUSTIN KATZ** is administrator of AnchorRising .com, an independent media and conservative analysis blog, and a monthly contributor to *Rhode Island Catholic*.

JAMES KIRCHICK is a contributing editor to the *New Republic*. He writes frequently for newspapers and magazines including the *Washington Post*, the *Wall Street Journal*, the *Los Angeles Times*, *Commentary*, *Policy Review*, and the *Weekly Standard*. He has been a columnist for the *Washington Examiner* and the *New York Daily News*. A contributing writer to the *Advocate*, the nation's largest gay publication, he is a recipient of the National Lesbian and Gay Journalists Association Journalist of the Year Award.

EVAN COYNE MALONEY directed the film *Indoctrinate U*, a shocking and humorous look at political correctness run amok on college campuses. Since 2001, he has edited Brain-Terminal.com, which hosts a number of his short videos. Evan's work has been covered by the *Wall Street Journal*, the *New York Times*, the *New York Post*, the *Washington Times*, *National Review*, and *The Weekly Standard*, among other publications. Evan has also appeared on CNN, Fox News, C-SPAN, CBN, and Comcast News.

KATHERINE MILLER is from McLean, Virginia, and graduated from Vanderbilt University in May 2010.

RACHEL MOTTE is a blogger, editor, and commentator on political and cultural issues at EvangelicalOutpost.com and RachelMotte.com. She graduated from the Torrey Honors Institute and Biola University with a degree in medieval history in 2004.

CAITRIN NICOL is managing editor of the *New Atlantis*.

MATT PATTERSON is a columnist and commentator and 2009–2010 National Review Institute Washington Fellow.

JOEL B. POLLAK is an author, speechwriter, and attorney, and the Republican nominee for Congress in the 9th district of Illinois in 2010.

JAMES POULOS is the managing editor of Ricochet.com. A doctoral candidate in government at Georgetown University, he is the founding editor of Postmodern Conservative, hosted at First Things. Previously, he was the political editor of Culture11. His writing has appeared online or in print at the *American Conservative*, the *American Spectator*, the *Boston Globe*, the *Guardian*, the *National Interest*, *The New Atlantic*, and *The Weekly Standard*, among other publications, and he is a regular contributor on Bloggingheads.

HELEN RITTELMEYER is an associate editor of *National Review*.

A 2009 Truman Scholar, Delaware native **BILL RIVERS** studies International Relations at the University of Delaware and is active in grassroots politics in the First State.

TODD SEAVEY's articles have appeared in publications ranging from *Reason* and *National Review* to *Spy* and Justice League of America comic books. He was an editor at the American Council on Science and Health. He blogs at ToddSeavey.com, hosts monthly bar debates in Manhattan, and is a writer-producer for the cable news organization that is not responsible for the views he expresses here.

BEN SHAPIRO is a Harvard Law School graduate, nationally syndicated columnist, and three-time bestselling author of *Brainwashed: How Universitites Indoctrinated Our Youth* (2004), *Porn Generation: How Social Liberalism Is Corrupting Our Future* (2005), and *Project President: Bad Hair and Botox on the Road to the White House* (2008). His next book will be published in 2011 by HarperCollins.

ASHLEY THORNE is the director of communications for the National Association of Scholars. She writes frequently about issues in higher education at www.nas.org. She received her undergraduate degree in politics, philosophy, and economics from the King's College in 2007, and she lives in Jersey City, New Jersey, with her husband.

MICHAEL WARREN, from Grayson, Georgia, graduated from Vanderbilt University in May 2010, and is a 2010–2011 Collegiate Newtwork Fellow at the *Weekly Standard*.

JOI WEAVER was classically educated at the Torrey Honors Institute and trained as an artist at Biola University; she currently resides in Southern California and blogs at EvangelicalOutpost.com and About-Face.org.